Hashtags and Headlines

Hashtags and Headlines

Marketing for School Leaders

Azure Angelov, Deidre Pettinga,
and David F. Bateman

ROWMAN & LITTLEFIELD
Lanham • Boulder • New York • London

Published by Rowman & Littlefield
An imprint of The Rowman & Littlefield Publishing Group, Inc.
4501 Forbes Boulevard, Suite 200, Lanham, Maryland 20706
www.rowman.com

6 Tinworth Street, London SE11 5AL, United Kingdom

British Library Cataloguing in Publication Information Available

Library of Congress Cataloging-in-Publication Data

ISBN 9781475853049 (cloth : alk. paper)
ISBN 9781475853056 (pbk. : alk. paper)
ISBN 9781475853063 (electronic)

∞^{TM} The paper used in this publication meets the minimum requirements of
American National Standard for Information Sciences—Permanence of Paper
for Printed Library Materials, ANSI/NISO Z39.48-1992.

Contents

An Unexpected Foreword

As we were meeting with educational leaders to collect case studies for this book, we sought out a few sentences from several for comments on the back cover. One principal submitted far more than a few sentences. His words captured the impetus for writing this book:

> One of the most important jobs a principal has is in marketing the school. Telling your school's story, communicating the vision, and explaining the "why" are the reasons this is such a critical task. In my opinion, marketing is the single most important vehicle in communicating the school's vision not just to parents and the community but, even more importantly, to our very own staff and students. It is the official description of who we are and why we are here, and even where we are going. It is where people see how your mission is implemented and viewed by those charged with carrying it out. It energizes our teachers and students to know that the community around us sees the great things they are doing!
>
> School leaders typically have no background or experience in marketing. We don't understand its usefulness. We also view it as somehow fake or like advertising. We don't understand that it is a powerful vehicle for telling our story, which is the truth! We generally depend on word of mouth as our only marketing tool, which takes care of itself. Unfortunately, with the nature of our business, many times word of mouth can work against a school more than for it. For example, a single negative experience can result in significant damage to a school's reputation due to the reach of social media. The positive stories and accomplishments sometimes struggle to be known. This book will help school leaders to begin to understand the importance and power that effective marketing

can have for a school, again, externally, but also internally among staff, students, and parents.

Dan Wilson
Principal, Lynhurst 7th and 8th Grade Center
2013 Indiana Middle School Principal of the Year

Introduction

From 1998 to 2004, the US Postal Service sponsored a professional cycling team. Many questioned the need for a federal agency to engage in marketing of any form. Here is an example of a complaint:

> Most federally-affiliated anything is likely so because the goods/services produced tend to serve a basic/commodity need. Hence added marketing in attempt to drive higher volumes seems unnecessary. It'd be like advertising the police department or a court system to boost the number of crimes reported or lawsuits filed. (ChicagoNow, 2013)

However, at about the same time, the US Postal Service had been losing market share, a trend that has continued (United States Postal Service, 2012). A US Post Office is unique in that no other place brings all of society together in the same way, and it seems hard to believe that an institution so central to American social and political life is losing cultural market share at roughly the same pace as newspapers and bookstores (Gelfand, 2012). The US Postal Service does much more than just deliver mail:

> Letter carriers serve as a kind of neighborhood watch; that postal workers help reestablish contact with citizens after natural disasters like Hurricane Katrina; and that the postal service plays a role in government services such as voter registration and census completion. (Wildlife officials in many Midwestern states, including Ohio, still rely on rural mail carrier surveys to estimate populations of everything from rabbits to quail.) Most strikingly, it pointed out the role that the Postal Service plays in nurturing social links, fostering civic pride, and "promoting community identity through local post offices and services that support civic engagement." (Gelfand, 2012)

1

US public schools are facing a similar decline. With competition from the various school choice options, the percentage of students attending public schools is dropping. But we need to realize that public schools, like the example above of the multifaceted US Postal Service, are more than just places for students to receive an education; they are the backbone of a community. They are a place for voting; a place for meeting; a place for Friday night football; the provider of educational services for the vast majority of the residents; a provider of breakfasts and lunches for less affluent children; a major stable employer of the community; the identity of the community. But this is changing.

Like the US Postal Service, which once held a virtual monopoly on the services they provided, public schools are losing market share, and with it many communities will be losing all the many important elements a public school provides.

A typical response from public school employees regarding marketing is viewing this as simply the need to tell their story. However, that is communication, and, while communication is an extremely important part of the marketing function, it is just a part of a bigger picture. Organizations that attempt to whittle the marketing function down solely to communication risk enormous failures. History is full of case studies where this has happened.

Consider, for example, Oldsmobile's attempt in the late 1980s to broaden its target audience to include younger car buyers. The carmaker's research identified that the majority of new car buyers were in the 20–30 age segment. However, most of those people viewed Oldsmobile as a brand for older people. To reach out to the younger buyers, Oldsmobile's advertising agency, Leo Burnett, developed what became a wildly successful ad campaign with the tagline, jingle, and television ads that featured the young adult children of well-recognized celebrities, such as Ringo Starr, Leonard Nimoy, William Shatner, and Harry Belafonte, among others. The popular ads brought young car buyers into Oldsmobile dealerships in droves to see the vehicle that was featured in the ads. Unfortunately, what they found was a product that had very few of the features they wanted and a price tag that was well above what they were able to afford. Although the ad campaign was deemed wildly popular with consumers, many business critics point to the overall marketing effort as the beginning of the end for Oldsmobile. The mishap highlights the notion that telling a good story is not enough. It showcases the simple truth: marketing is much more than communication.

Historically, public school systems in the United States have had a virtual monopoly on the provision of educational services across the country. Educators never had to worry about getting new students—they always had a steady supply. However, times have changed. Due to declining resources for public schools, changing demographics, vouchers, and heightened scrutiny over test scores—coupled with an explosion in the number of alternative and private schools—public schools in the US are facing uncharted waters. They are, in many ways, completely unprepared for an evolution that has been forced upon them.

With this changing educational landscape, public perception of public schools is dismal in many areas. Newspapers often focus their coverage of public schools on low test scores, crimes at schools, accidents on school buses, demands for better (or more) teacher pay, and the occasional need to talk about raising taxes to pay for schools generally characterized as mismanaged. The only good news a public school might get is a description of the success of a sports team, though that is often left to the whims of the sports editor of the local paper.

Public schools do many good things and play a vital role in our society. Unfortunately, people don't seem to know this part of the story. Public schools tend to have wider courses of study, more qualified teachers, guidance services, transportation, more extracurricular activities, social services, and special education services, and, due to their larger sizes, they often offer the students a richer experience, which helps prepare them for life.

In spite of this, public school employees have tremendous difficulty making the local community aware of the good things happening in their public schools—all the while recognizing it is the positive facets of the public school system that help distinguish it in the face of growing competition. However, just knowing the story isn't enough. Public school employees are not helpless victims of today's education policies; they are in fact, the valiant defenders of the future of public education.

While it has not been a skill set traditionally or explicitly taught, public school employees must become masters of their own destiny. Today's public school employees need to understand why, when, where, and how to market their schools to continue to serve our communities in this changing educational climate.

One of the biggest shifts in thinking that must take place is for public school employees to begin to see that, in today's society, there is competition for students and therefore there is a need to think about how to market their school. To market their school, public school employees are going to have to understand what they do well, understand what the others have to offer, and change their thinking about getting information out to others.

This ideological shift is a difficult one to make and can initially leave passionate educators feeling defeated. If public schools are going to thrive in today's society, it is necessary to recognize and respond to the current field of education. It is professionally naive to sit idly by and wish for the good old days or maintain the status quo, rather than evolving to the reality while working toward the future educators believe is possible.

One of the most important factors in marketing a school or any product, for that matter, is understanding the customer. Due to the changing competitive landscape in education, it is becoming vital to understand how families select schools for their children. No longer is it just enrolling the child in the closest school and hope all goes well. Families today are shopping for schools in a manner similar to the way they research a new appliance or automobile prior to purchase.

Unfortunately, many public schools are unprepared to assist families in this decision-making process. Public schools need new tools to navigate the changing dynamics of education. They need to engage with families and their communities when developing new programs or choosing which programs to close; understand the reasons for telling others about what they do; and then work, using new media and old, to develop a comprehensive and coherent strategy for successfully marketing their program. That is the purpose of this book.

A school principal can't just tell a secretary to put out a press release to the local paper. A superintendent can no longer ask a district-level communications specialist to just communicate all of the good things going on. Much more is expected, and it needs be part of a unified plan. The lines between marketing and public relations have blurred for public schools, and what may have worked in the past may not be the best now. The most obvious route may also not help achieve the ultimate goal, helping to successfully market a school or program.

This innovative book, *Hashtags and Headlines*, provides educators with clear and concise strategies to develop their marketing skill set and solve daily problems facing public schools across the country. The authors come from a public school background and a marketing background, and they understand the complexity of needs facing public schools that have to do more with less. While there are numerous business-book models on how to market a product, this book is unique in that it describes effective strategies and techniques for specifically marketing public education to the community.

There is really nothing like it out there—a book written jointly by educators and a marketer serving as a primer on marketing a school. Families, school boards, community members, and policy makers need a balanced understanding to draw from when making decisions about public schools. In order for this to happen, public educators must become more savvy and strategic at marketing their programs in this complex competitive environment.

Today's administrators need to understand why, when, where, and how to market their schools to continue to serve their communities in this changing educational climate. One of the biggest shifts in thinking that must take place is for educators to begin to see that, in today's society, there is competition for students. This competitive environment calls for educators to appreciate the need to market their school.

To be successful in this endeavor, public school educators have to understand what they do well and what their communities want from them, identify what their competitors have to offer, and, most importantly, change their beliefs that marketing and communication are synonymous. If public schools are going to thrive in today's competitive environment, they must recognize and respond to current market conditions.

REFERENCES

ChicagoNow. (2013, April 23). Why did the USPS sponsor Lance Armstrong anyway? Retrieved from http://www.chicagonow.com/cinnamon-twists/2013/04/why-did-the-usps-sponsor-lance-armstrong-anyway/.

Gelfand, A. (2012). Bye, bye, USPS? Denison Magazine. Retrieved from http://denisonmagazine.com/2012/features/bye-bye-usps/.

United States Postal Service. (2012, February 16). Plan to profitability: 5 year business plan. Retrieved from http://about.usps.com/news/national-releases/2012/pr12_0217profitability.pdf.

Chapter One

Relationship Building with Educational Consumers

Marketing is a core part of anything you do.

—Keith Belling, Founder and Chairman of Popchips

Parents often want what is best for their child. What they do is to use the internet to research the schools in their area. Before you go any further in this book, do the following:

1. Google "schools."
2. Better yet, Google "good schools." The results you will come up with will likely include the following:

   a. K–12 online school
   b. DeVry Tech
   c. Virtual or charter schools
   d. Best high schools under US News and World Report
   e. A guide for choosing schools in the UK that have embedded advertisements for K–12 online schools

You would be very unlikely to find your school (if you were to find your school, it would likely be due to a sports score). Now, if you Google "great schools," you will find GreatSchools.org and find your school compared to others around you with each of you given a rating based on a variety of quantifiable indicators (data).

Parents are now searching for schools in ways unheard of 15 or 25 years ago, and there is a competitive marketplace for education, in large part as a result of the internet, that public school employees are completely unprepared for.

A public school administrator's typical response is to put out a press release extolling the latest test scores hoping it will be placed in the local newspaper. Even if that does get published, who reads it? What does it really say about your school? Are decision-makers paying attention to that story? Are parents? Does it really level the playing field with all information available from other schools?

Typically, many school administrators and teachers think marketing is sending out a press release. Does a single press release market your school? Do businesses send out a single press release to market their business? This book is about marketing for public school employees, not how to compose a press release.

WHAT DOES THIS MEAN FOR PUBLIC SCHOOL EMPLOYEES?

For many educators, discussing education as a product and the landscape of public education as a marketplace is very much an ideological shift. While much of the debate about school choice and competition has focused on the positives and negatives of these types of educational systems, this book takes a different perspective. This book is not supporting or combating competition or choice movements. It does, however, recognize that public schools currently function within a competitive environment and therefore educators will need to change.

This book is meant to serve as a tool for public educators to navigate competitive waters. Marketing education is not a negative, and it really is not in contrast to the overall mission of public education. A more specific understanding of the role marketing plays in public education is a vital next step for educators in their pursuit of innovation and evolution. To move forward, public educators must embrace a proactive role in deliberately sharing the importance of what is provided to students and communities while recognizing many others in town (and online) offer similar services.

Some history. Public education in the US started in the 1800s. It was originally established as part of the Department of War when it became apparent the country could not sustain an effective military with large numbers of illiterate soldiers (Cross, 2010). Over the years public education grew in size and mission, reflecting the changes of the nation. Since its creation, public education has served a variety of purposes for our society. For decades, public education has produced citizens who make informed decisions when voting and participating in conversations related to the role of government.

For many Americans, it was the opportunity for a free public education that provided them the tools they needed to change their lives. Public education has produced students with the will and drive to become whatever their hearts and minds chose. Public education has produced generations of taxpayers who are able to provide for themselves and others. The true impact of our product, a free public education, is virtually immeasurable.

For public schools to truly move forward, public school employees must recognize it is their obligation to learn how to be masters of their own destiny and share their work in a way that educates others of the value of a public education. As public schools find themselves yet again facing the expectations of an evolving society, it is important to recognize it is not the only profession that has needed to embrace marketing as a means to grow.

Several other public entities have embraced the importance of marketing strategies as competition entered their fields. In 1973, the Department of Defense became an all-volunteer organization and began its first marketing campaign to educate the public on their services and opportunities (Cross, 2010). These efforts still continue today and offer the public an alternative understanding of the military experience from those portrayed by popular media. In the face of technological advances and competitive markets, public libraries have also turned to marketing strategies to continue to pursue their mission (Robinson, 2012).

Public libraries have determined that to thrive they must make sure the public understands what they provide and center their efforts on being more user focused. One of the most notable public entities that have strong ties with marketing campaigns is the US Postal Service. In the age of the internet and email, the US Postal Service recognized a disconnect between the way customers saw mail and utilized large-scale marketing campaigns to inform the public of their services (Hudgins, 2001). As each of these entities began to move forward, one of the first steps was for them to recognize how what was expected of them has changed.

As public schools look to the future, they must recognize the changes in the societal landscape and decide what this means. Private schools in the US began in the 16th century as missionary entities. Many private schools across the country have maintained these religious roots and their own identities outside of public forums, leaving a very dichotomous existence between the two. The lines between public and private education were very clear, and bureaucratic systems were in place based on these boundaries.

The recent legislative push for choice and competition has muddied these once clear waters. Public education is now one piece of a much larger and more complex educational marketplace. As the marketplace has changed, so must the behaviors of public schools and their employees.

The field of educational research has spent a considerable amount of energy examining the relationship between schools and families. Much of this research has focused on understanding what schools can do to partner with families to support the academic achievement of their students. In this new era of choice and competition, understanding and building relationships with families is only part of the story. Public schools now need to know why families choose their school, why they stay, and why they leave.

From a marketing perspective, we must begin to examine the relationship between the public school and the community through the lens of the value exchange model. This perspective allows public schools a more holistic view of the relationship they engage in with the community, as well as the services they provide communities and families in exchange for their tax dollars.

Public schools have been rightfully focused on the product they provide. Many conversations are about test scores and other singular measures of success of schools. This post–industrial revolution era perspective on marketing is known as a product concept of marketing. Public educators have been focused on sharing only one aspect of the services they provide, many times in a reactionary fashion. To thrive in the educational marketplace of today, public education must begin to engage with a societal concept of marketing. To begin our understanding of public school marketing, it is important to understand what marketing is and how it has evolved.

As is the case in a variety of industries today, educators are being pulled in a number of directions. Trite as it may sound, they are being challenged to wear a number of different hats and, in general, accomplish more with less. The changing landscape has forced administrators and teachers to understand concepts related to business and marketing, which are generally outside the scope of their academic background and professional expertise. Schools today are being asked to market themselves but are not given the instruction on what it means to market a school, let alone the resources to do it properly.

Most people think they have a general understanding of what marketing is all about because, as consumers, we've been exposed to a wide variety of marketing communications efforts in the form of advertisements, sales pitches, and other promotional activities. However, marketing communications is just a subset of marketing, a discipline encompassing far more than the act of producing an ad or sponsoring an event.

The development of marketing as a discipline has been an outgrowth of how business has evolved over the past 150 years. In the post–industrial revolution era, business management has changed its philosophy a number of times on how to sell a product to a customer (Armstrong & Kotler, 2013; Kotler, 1988). In early industrial times, management tended to operate under the production concept, believing consumers would buy goods that are readily available and highly affordable. As a result, the focus of the operation was on producing goods at such a level needed to realize economies of scale, thereby making the goods both available and affordable.

This concept is operationally successful as long as demand exceeds supply. However, as competition grew and a number of different organizations were able to produce and sell similar goods at affordable prices, business managers shifted their thinking to what is known as the product concept. While this philosophy still emphasizes mass production, it states consumers will favor the superior good; therefore, emphasis should be placed on continually improving the product to gain a competitive advantage.

By the early 1900s there were a number of businesses producing goods—leading to excess supply. This was coupled by an economic recession, causing a decrease in demand. With inventories piling up, management philosophy changed yet again, resulting in the selling concept, which holds consumers will not buy goods unless the firm undertakes a large-scale selling and promotional effort. It was in this period the traveling salesman was born (Solomon, 2004). However, none of the managerial concepts to date placed much emphasis on the consumer. Designing, producing, and selling products were more important. It wasn't until the post–World War II era that companies started to think about the consumer. The era of the marketing concept ushered in a focus on understanding the needs of the customer.

This philosophy holds that only by satisfying the needs and wants of the consumer will an organization be successful. The marketing concept is still practiced today, though it has evolved to some extent to what is referred to as the holistic or societal marketing concept, which still stresses the importance of meeting consumers' needs but doing it in such a way to benefit not only the consumer but society as well. Green marketing and sustainable marketing practices are examples of the societal marketing concept.

Along with the evolution of business management philosophies, the definition of marketing has also changed over time. The American Marketing Association (AMA) is credited with developing the first official definition of marketing back in 1938, after the US Census Bureau requested the association's help in providing a consistent definition of marketing to be used by all government agencies. While the definition has changed a number of times (with another review taking place in 2012–2013), the AMA's current definition of marketing follows: "Marketing is the activity, set of institutions, and processes for creating, communicating, delivering, and exchanging offerings that have value for customers, clients, partners, and society at large" (Armstrong & Kotler, 2013; Smith, 1956).

Central to this definition is the notion of the value exchange, a concept educators really need to understand. In other words, businesses aren't merely producing goods and selling them to people. Rather, they are giving up something of value (the good) in exchange for something else of value (money, in most cases). Viewed in this light, we can begin to understand the importance of consumers to the equation. Buyers are not simply getting something from the seller; they are giving up something to get something in return. In education, residents of the district are giving up something (taxes) in exchange for something else (education for the students).

In most cases what they give up is, in fact, money, though that isn't always the case. For example, if a person makes a donation of a pint of blood to a blood bank, one might think there is no exchange. Although the blood bank receives the donated blood, the consumer does, in fact, get something back: a sense of goodwill or satisfaction for having done something worthwhile, not to mention a cookie and a glass of orange juice! The two parties have exchanged something of value. This is often the selling point for educators, that we are doing something good by paying taxes; however, not every person is pleased about paying taxes.

We can begin to think of marketing as an exchange that occurs between the buyer and the seller, shown in Figure 1.1.

As the marketing model illustrates, the two parties come together to trade items of worth or significance. For the seller, the item produced doesn't always have to be a good or service—like a pair of shoes or a haircut. As demonstrated in the blood bank example, the value blood banks provide consumers has nothing to do with any manufactured item. The marketers at the American Red Cross, for example, focus on the benefits of giving blood with how good it feels to donate and that it will help ensure there is enough blood available for people in need (American Red Cross, 2013).

Likewise for the buyer, the thing that is given up isn't always measured in terms of money. It can be a donation of time or blood or even a vote for a particular political candidate. People cast their vote with the hope that it will result in the kind of representation they want in a particular public office. Value exchanges can exist on many levels, and they are at the root of marketing.

With this in mind, we offer a more streamlined definition of marketing, one centered on the concept of the value exchange. We believe marketing can be defined as "All those activities that facilitate the exchange of value between the buyer and the seller." As we will discuss in Chapter 3, the "activities" facilitating the value exchange can be broken down into four areas: product, price, place, and promotion, or the marketing mix. These

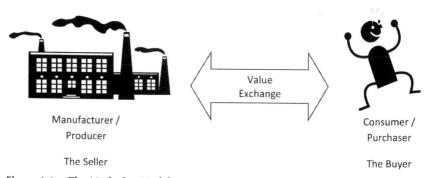

Manufacturer /
Producer

Value
Exchange

Consumer /
Purchaser

The Seller

The Buyer

Figure 1.1. The Marketing Model

are generally referred to as the 4*P*s. Other sources have suggested the inclusion of additional *P*s, such as people, processes, philosophy, and a variety of others.

However, for the discussion of public school marketing, we will confine our definition to include the traditional 4*P*s. While the marketing model and definition are admittedly simple at this point, throughout the book we will layer in additional concepts that will help broaden the reader's understanding of marketing.

Finally, it should be stressed that although the marketing model showcases one seller and one buyer, in reality, there are multiple buyers and sellers. In nearly every aspect of their purchasing lives, consumers have a variety of options available to them. Likewise, sellers do not simply produce and sell a single good to one customer. If that were the case, it would be quite simple for a business to understand what a purchaser wants and customize a solution for that particular individual. Today, most goods are mass-produced for a large audience—a collection of consumers who have a lot of competitors vying for their attention and money.

The rare exception to the competitive environment is found in the case of a monopoly, such as an electric utility. To some extent, public school systems have had, until recently, territorial monopolies. Good school systems in the right part of town continually flourished because people wanted to buy a house in that area so their children could go to the schools in that district. However, the environment has shifted, and hence the need for this book. Traditional public schools have found themselves in an increasingly competitive arena with charter schools, vouchers, private schools, online education, and interdistrict choice programs becoming more widespread.

POSITIONING

As noted above, the marketing relationship between the seller and the buyer does not happen in a vacuum. There are a variety of other competitors targeting consumers with similar or even different offers. By different offers, we must recognize that nearly all buyers have a fixed limit on the amount of disposable income they can or will spend on a certain activity, say leisure-time fun. The number of leisure-time fun opportunities where consumers could spend their money is practically endless—ranging from weekend getaways, to movies, to bowling, and so forth.

The number of competing categories is vast, and the number of options within each category may or may not have a large number of competitors in it. For example, on any given weekend, there are generally many different movies playing, whereas in a small town, there may be only one bowling alley. The point is marketers need to consider both their direct and indirect competition and monitor the impact that both sets of competitors have on their business. The next section discusses the competitive marketplace from the consumer's perspective and how to successfully distinguish an organization within that landscape.

To effectively market a product, one must first identify the target. For educators, this would be students to come to their school. A target market is a set of consumers who share a common need or other characteristics the organization wishes to serve (Armstrong & Kotler, 2013). The common need or characteristic used to identify a market segment can be based on a number of variables. These include geographic, demographic, psychographic, and behavioral (Kotler, 1988). Geographic area can include regions of the country, urban versus rural areas, or even particular climates.

Demographic variables consist of age, sex, family size, income, occupation, education, religion, ability, race, and nationality. Psychographic variables combine psychological, sociological, and anthropological characteristics, such as social class, lifestyle (such as outdoorsmen or scrapbookers), or personality (such as ambitious or frugal) (Solomon, 2004). Behavioral variables an organization may want to consider as a basis for market segmentation include purchase occasions (such as holidays or anniversaries), user status (such as potential user, current user, ex-user), usage rate (such as heavy or light user), and attitude toward the product (ranging from enthusiastic to hostile).

An organization should identify which segments exist and then select the one or ones they believe are the most viable. A viable market segment is one with measurable purchasing power, is large enough to remain profitable, can be readily accessed and served by the organization, and will actively respond to the marketing effort.

Once a segment is selected, there are three basic options to target the segment: very broadly (undifferentiated marketing), very narrowly (niche or micromarketing), or somewhere in the middle (differentiated or concentrated marketing) (Smith, 1956). An undifferentiated marketing effort is one in which the organization ignores any differences that may exist among segments and targets the entire market with one offer. The marketing mix strategy targets everyone. Examples range from basic food staples to postage stamps; the product and the way it is marketed to people is all the same.

At the other end of the spectrum is niche or micromarketing. Here, the organization identifies a small segment not currently being served by other competitors. This could be a local marketing effort or even individualized or custom marketing. This is more common in professional services marketing, such as architecture or legal services where "product" solutions and even the marketing messages are tailored specifically to individual clients.

However, in the business-to-consumer realm, an example can be found in real estate sales, where sales representatives customize a set of homes to show to clients based on their individual needs and preferences. Where schools are concerned, examples of niches include charter or private schools targeting specific student populations, like students with exceptional needs.

Differentiated or concentrated marketing falls in between undifferentiated and niche marketing. Here, organizations serve multiple segments, each with a specific marketing mix of product, price, place, and promotion. An example includes Hilton Hotels, whose portfolio of brands includes, among others, the luxury Conrad Hilton Hotels, Hilton Garden Inn with more of a residential atmosphere for business travelers, and the midlevel, value-priced Hampton Inn (Hilton Worldwide, 2013). The product offerings are designed to serve different segments, and the price points vary. In addition, the placement of a Conrad Hilton Hotel is more likely to be either in the heart of a large metropolitan area or at a destination location, such as an island resort.

Conversely, a Hampton Inn is more readily situated off an interstate exchange. Finally, the strategies used to promote each brand use different messaging and media strategies. The Hampton Inn, which targets a larger traveling segment, such as middle-class families, is more likely to advertise on the mass medium of television than the Conrad brand. As can be seen from these examples, the marketing mix used is a function of the target segment the organization wishes to serve.

At least from a product perspective, most traditional public schools could be characterized as falling within the differentiated segment strategy. Naturally, school systems target children by age—with elementary, middle, and high schools. However, additional programs target specific populations; examples include vocational training and special education, as well as GED and international baccalaureate programs, among others.

Beyond identifying a segment to serve and selecting a targeting strategy, the organization must select a value proposition, which helps distinguish the brand from the competition (Armstrong & Kotler, 2013). The value proposition also helps consumers identify the value of the potential exchange. In other words, by knowing the value of the product or service, buyers can decide the level of value they would need to exchange to obtain it. To organize the variety of options available in any one category, consumers use mental cues to help them distinguish one product from another. Recognizing this, marketers must develop a positioning strategy to help influence consumers' understanding of the product's value proposition (Solomon, 2004).

Positioning allows the organization to design the brand's image and value proposition so the buyers in the target segment appreciate the distinguishing features of the brand, relative to the competition. For any one category, an organization can research consumers' perceptions of competitors based on key distinguishing factors, such as customer service or luxury, by using a perceptual map. Figure 1.2 shows an example of how consumers might

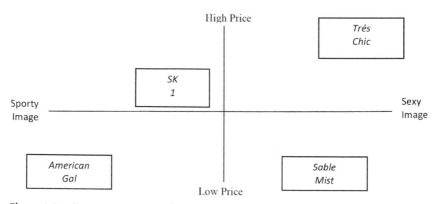

Figure 1.2. Fragrance Perceptual Map

evaluate a series of fictitious women's fragrances based on key variables of price (plotted on the *Y*-axis) and image (plotted on the *X*-axis).

Generally speaking, a product can distinguish itself in two ways: price and differentiation (Porter, 1980). Competitors seeking to engage in price competition are typically larger organizations with considerable market share who are able to enjoy the kind of economies of scale resulting in lower production and operating costs. Organizations operating under these conditions are generally able to charge a lower price and are in a better position to compete effectively when additional competitors wage price wars against them. It should be recognized the price and cost-structure model that exists within the public schools category is unique. These distinctive characteristics will be discussed in greater detail.

Beyond price, a brand can also position itself based on a unique differentiating characteristic, such as customer service, styling, or performance. Results of perceptual mapping research can assist marketers with establishing an effective positioning strategy. As Reis and Trout argued, positioning allows marketers to establish a stake-hold or frame of reference in the mind of the consumer (Ries & Trout, 1982).

An effectively established and articulately communicated position strategy needs to be rooted in a positioning statement. A positioning statement summarizes the brand's positioning by identifying the target segment and its need, the brand concept, and the point of difference (Calder & Reagan, 2001). Below are several examples of product positioning statements.

- Zipcar: "To urban-dwelling, educated techno-savvy consumers [target], when you use Zipcar car-sharing service instead of owning a car [brand concept], you save money while reducing your carbon footprint [points of difference]" (Armstrong & Kotler, 2013).
- BlackBerry: "To busy, mobile professionals who always need to be in the loop [target], the BlackBerry is a wireless business connectivity solution [brand concept] that gives you an easier, more reliable way to stay connected to data, people, and resources while on the go [points of difference]" (Armstrong & Kotler, 2013).

It should be noted that a positioning statement should not be confused with a mission statement. A mission statement details the organization's purpose or reason for existence. Positioning statements identify a product's membership within a particular category and distinguish the unique characteristics of the product, which differentiate it from other competing brands found in the same category. For example, global consumer products giant Proctor & Gamble has the following mission:

> We will provide branded products and services of superior quality and value that improve the lives of the world's consumers, now and for generations to come. As a result, consumers will reward us with leadership sales, profit and value creation, allowing our people, our shareholders and the communities in which we live and work to prosper. (Purpose, Values & Principles, n.d.)

However, the company's website details the 50 brands the company produces and distributes. In terms of the target segment being served, the product concept, and the points of difference, the Pampers brand is positioned quite differently from Cover Girl or Head & Shoulders. Organizations need mission statements, as well as positioning statements.

Many schools develop mission statements such as the following:

> Kitty Hawk Elementary School (NC) seeks to create a challenging learning environment that encourages high expectations for success through development-appropriate instruction that allows for individual differences and learning styles. Our school promotes a safe, orderly, caring, and supportive environment. Each student's self-esteem is fostered by positive relationships with students and staff. We strive to have our parents, teachers, and community members actively involved on our students' learning.

> City High School (TX) strives to be a community of learners in which all members use their minds well and care about one another. We engage with challenging academics and the unique resources of our city and region in order to become active citizens and responsible stewards of our world.

> The Scott M. Ellis Elementary School (SC) community is committed to active, reflective, creative learning. We believe learning is maximized when it takes place in an environment enriched with support, encouragement and assistance. We celebrate the pursuit of lifelong learning and are committed to nurturing high self-esteem and respect for others. We believe that everyone can learn, become better thinkers and independent learners. An integral

part of our learning process will have our school community learning how to ask questions, solve problems and make thoughtful decisions.

The mission of Harbordale Elementary School (FL) is to ensure every student's intellectual and emotional growth and to promote effective citizenship. We will offer a diversity of curriculum and cultural experiences that meet the individual needs of our students through a school-wide and community effort.

The mission of Ridgedale Middle School (NJ), in partnership with the community, is to provide students with the skills and exploratory experiences that enable them to reach their fullest potential as independent thinkers. By providing a diversified curriculum and a school environment that foster civic mindedness, self-esteem and respect for individual differences, we seek to address the unique needs of the early adolescent in a changing society.

The Capital Area Intermediate Unit, Enola, Pennsylvania. The mission of the Capital Area Intermediate Unit is to achieve educational excellence with our families, schools, and communities, through leadership, partnership, and innovation.

As you can see, these mission statements are clearly different from a positioning statement. As will be discussed further in this book, the product's positioning should serve as a guiding frame of reference for all decisions related to the marketing mix. For example, take the format of a positioning statement; it's quite straightforward. It doesn't read or sound like a jingle or commercial slogan. Nonetheless, the positioning statement can (and should) be used to guide the development of an appropriate commercial message.

Several years ago, the UPS Company featured an advertising slogan that read "We run the tightest ship in the shipping business." This cleverly worded play on words effectively communicated the company's positioning of superior logistics capabilities ("UPS's Values, Mission and Strategy," n.d.). Managers should continually refer to the positioning statement to ensure all aspects of the marketing mix uphold the product's positioning, beginning with the product. Therefore, organizations need to make sure that the product or service they are delivering to consumers actually *delivers* on the value proposition.

WHAT DO OUTSIDERS "KNOW"
ABOUT YOUR SCHOOL?

Most of the research and dialogue about the relationship between families and public schools has focused on partnerships between the two groups with intentions of improving the academic performance of students (Henderson, Mapp, Johnson, & Davies, 2007). In some cases, this research also discusses the role public schools can play in communities and notes the importance of teachers living within the communities they serve (Murrell, 2001). The crux of much of this work focuses on the personal relationships and interactions between educators and families.

As public educators think about their relationship with families and the larger community, they must also understand they are funded by tax dollars and essentially work for taxpayers. Public schools provide a public service to the larger community, as well as to individual families. From a marketing perspective, it is important for public schools to identify and understand the viable market segment they serve.

Previously, public schools have had a certain group of students they served based on geographic location. In many ways, public schools held the lion's share of power in their relationships with families because they were the only option for many families. In a competitive market, this is no longer the case. Families that previously had very few options are now bombarded with many choices. Research has shown schools often offer services and programs for families based on what they believe families need, rather than by collecting data from families to find out what they want (Smiley, Howland, & Anderson, 2008).

Working from inaccurate assumptions about a community often leads to low levels of family participation and tensions between schools and families. Public schools must begin to analyze data about the communities they serve as closely as they analyze data on student achievement. In a landscape of choice, identifying the families to be served and their expectations of public schools is important. Public schools must begin to focus on the families in their community that utilize or will utilize public education options in their communities.

Once families are identified that will most likely choose a public school option for their children, it is important to collect data on how they perceive the school. Here are some questions that will help:

- What is the reputation of the public school in the community?
- When families describe their experience with the school to their neighbors, what do they say?
- What do realtors tell potential homebuyers in the community about the school?
- What do pediatricians tell their patients about the public school?
- What type of media coverage has the public school received in the past several years?
- How do the alumni describe their experience with the school?
- What do employers, other schools, or colleges say about the graduates?
- After collecting these types of data, educators must begin to decipher the validity of these perceptions. Are they the perceptions one wants families and communities to have about the school?
- Are there any perceptions that are surprises?

Not all of the questions are important, but each will assess the viable market segment and perceptions of the school and understand the competition.

Public schools have a long history of working with the private schools within their jurisdictions. In many capacities, public and private schools have worked together to serve their communities. Both entities have provided a necessary service, and the relationship between both types of schools was fairly clear cut. Each type of school served a different student population within their community, so competition was of little concern. Now that various types of publicly funded schools are competing for the same students, it is important to identify the public school options families have in the jurisdiction. Here are some questions that will help with the identification:

- Which public schools in the area are targeting the same families?
- Once the competition is identified, it is important to begin to develop an understanding of what they offer families. Why do families choose those schools?
- Why do they stay in those schools?
- Why do they leave those schools?
- How do families and the community perceive those schools?
- What type of media coverage have those schools received in the past few years?

- How do alumni describe their experience with that school?
- What do employers, other schools, or colleges say about their graduates?

After collecting perception data on the school and the competition, one can begin to understand the competitive landscape. At this point there needs to begin the development of an appropriate marketing mix for the targeted market segment. It is helpful to develop a value proposition grid based on the public perception of the school and the competition. Plot the school and the competition schools on the map. Figure 1.3 shows an example of how educational consumers might evaluate competitor schools based on extracurricular options (plotted on the Y-axis) and academic achievement (plotted on the X-axis).

By distinguishing the school from its competitors in this manner, one can develop a positioning statement aligning with the mission statement. Keep in mind the positioning statement is a frame of reference for the families and community. Additionally, the positioning strategy should be deeply rooted in the positioning statement. It must convey to the target market segment both brand concept and points differentiating the school

Public School Perceptual Map

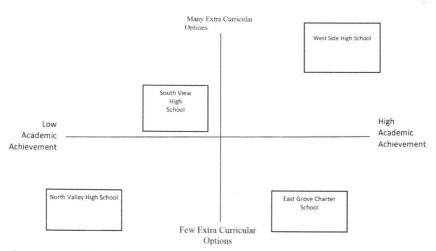

Figure 1.3.   Public School Perceptual Map

from the competition. Below are a few examples of public school positioning statements:

- West Side High School: "To highly educated, sport-savvy families [target], when you choose to send your child to West Side High School instead of a charter [brand concept], you provide your child with an academically rigorous and athletically competitive experience [points of difference]."
- East Grove Charter School: "To academically focused families who want their children to focus on intellectual pursuits [target], an East Grove education provides academic experiences and consultants [brand concept] that offer your student a superior foundation in academics and an easier transition into a prestigious university [points of difference]."

Both of these examples can work in tandem with the mission statement of the school and as part of the strategic plan. A positioning statement allows educators to synthesize their perceptual data in a meaningful way for families as they make educational choices. The importance for public schools to begin to tell their own stories cannot be overstated. Recently, public education has been the subject of popular media, Hollywood movies, and legislative efforts. Public education has ample opportunity to grow in their efforts to strategically tell their own story and offer an alternate view from those offered by various media outlets.

The focus of local and national news outlets is to provide quick snapshots of newsworthy events within their community. Mainstream movies are meant to entertain and generate profits. Neither of these entities is meant to tell the story of public education. Educators have allowed these entities too much power in shaping public opinion about the service they provide communities. By being proactive, outspoken, thoughtful, and strategic about sharing the benefits of public education to the larger communities, educators can begin to offer a more informed and authentic perspective.

CASE STUDY:
Beware of Unintended Consequences

As school leaders navigate their way through the environmental forces brought on by charter schools, vouchers, and online educational options, it can be difficult to predict the impact of any particular action in the ever-changing, competitive marketplace. There are a number of examples where marketing efforts have realized consequences that were both unforeseen and unintended.

An effort in the early 2000s by the Center City Schools Initiative (CCSI) in Philadelphia sought to rebrand the urban schools in Center City region of the School District of Philadelphia. CCSI was a partnership between the school district and the local business improvement district, formed for the purpose of attracting upper-middle-class, professional families to live and enroll their children in the public schools of the Center City (Cucchiara, 2008).

Traditionally, the urban schools had struggled with student achievement. Marketing the inner-city schools to well-educated professionals, who were more inclined to send their children to private or high-performing charter schools, called for the district to change their market position. The result was a distinctive branding for the Center City Schools as academies, setting them apart even from the other schools in the school district. The efforts were intentionally geared toward upper-middle-class parents, who were viewed as highly desirable and valued customers, and thereby ignoring low-income (and often minority) families. The efforts to promote urban renewal and revitalize the schools were successful. However, they carry with them some powerful unintended consequences, namely, that they exacerbate "the effects of race, class, and geography on students' educational experiences and opportunities" (Cucchiara, 2008, p. 176).

A study conducted by Turner (2018) of two Wisconsin school districts showed that, despite marketing efforts that emphasized the racial diversity of the student population, school leaders tend to aim their marketing efforts at White upper- and middle-class families. Turner's work "Raises difficult questions about how marketing diversity may perpetuate White racial hierarchy" (p. 811), as the presence, interests, and cultures of students of color were promoted as a benefit to the educational experiences of White students. The unintended consequence:

"When Whites determine the value of the identities of people of color in relation to their own benefit, the racial status hierarchy is reinforced" (Leong, 2013, as cited in Turner, 2018, p. 812).

Beyond the ethical considerations that result from the unintended consequences of marketing activities, school leaders must also be aware of the very real legal risks tied to K–12 educational marketing. In 2018, an Indianapolis family filed suit against Indianapolis Public Schools, claiming the district engaged in deceptive advertising practices (Herron, 2018). The family claimed the school district overstated its connection to a Butler University in its marketing materials, leading them to believe their son would have access to tuition-free, college-level courses at the private university. Failure for the high school to deliver the college-level course resulted in the parents incurring out-of-pocket expenses to enroll their son at a local state-operated Indiana university, Purdue University at Indianapolis. The family stated that, had they known their son would not have access to courses at Butler, they would not have enrolled him at Shortridge High School.

According to the Federal Trade Commission, which regulates advertising as a part of its consumer protection responsibilities, it is incumbent on the organization marketing its programs and services to the public to engage in advertising practices that are truthful, evidence based, and in no way deceptive or unfair ("Advertising and Marketing," n.d.).

Finally, school marketing has implications for students as well. An examination of marketing practices in England reveals that, while some parents may be more discerning consumers when searching for a school, children may not. Marketing of education was first permitted in England in the early 1990s (Norris, 2016). Operating in a competitive environment, secondary schools, in particular, focused their marketing efforts on attracting high-performing students. One of the most common tactics is an open house event for students transitioning into secondary school, featuring abbreviated lessons for prospective students. The unintended consequence of such events is they tend to mislead students, creating unrealistic expectations, which result in disappointment or diminished self-confidence for students who are unable to meet the performance standards (Abrahams, 2007).

While today's school leaders find themselves operating in a competitive environment, the overall marketing plan needs to consider the ethical, legal, and emotional implications of the tactics being employed in order to avoid unintended consequences.

REFERENCES

Abrahams, I. (2007). An unrealistic image of science. *School Science Review*, *88*, 119–122.

Advertising and Marketing. (n.d.). Retrieved from https://www.ftc.gov/tips-advice/business-center/advertising-and-marketing.

American Marketing Association. (2007). Definitions of marketing (approved October 2007). Retrieved from https://www.ama.org/the-definition-of-marketing-what-is-marketing/.

American Red Cross. (2013). Benefits of donating. Retrieved from http://www.redcrossblood.org/donating-blood.

Armstrong, G., & Kotler, P. (2013). *Marketing: An introduction* (11th ed.). Boston, MA: Pearson.

Calder, B., & Reagan, S. (2001). Brand design. In D. Iacobucci (Ed.), *Kellogg on marketing* (pp. 61). New York, NY: John Wiley & Sons.

Cross, C. T. (2010). *Political education: National policy comes of age.* New York, NY: Teachers College Press.

Cucchiara, M. (2008). Re-branding urban schools: Urban revitalization, social status, and marketing public schools to the upper middle class. *Journal of Education Policy, 23*(2), 165–179.

Friedman, W. A. (2004). *Birth of a salesman: The transformation of selling in America.* Cambridge, MA: Harvard University Press.

Henderson, A. T., Mapp, K. L., Johnson, V. R., & Davies, D. (2007). *Beyond the bake sale.* New York, NY: The New Press.

Herron, A. (2018, November 28). Family sues IPS for "deceptive" marketing of Shortridge High School. *The Indianapolis Star*. Retrieved from https://www.indystar.com/story/news/education/2018/11/28/family-sues-ips-deceptive-marketing-shortridge-high-school-indianapolis-school-choice/2131041002/.

Hilton Worldwide. (2013). Summary of brands. Retrieved from http://www.hiltondevelopment.com/dl/HiltonWorldwide_portfolio_brochure.en.

Hudgins, E. L. (2001). *Mail @ the Millennium: Will the postal service go private?* Washington, DC: Cato Institute.

Kotler, P. (1988). *Marketing management: Analysis, planning, implementation, and control* (6th ed.). Englewood Cliffs, NJ: Prentice Hall.

Kotler, P. (2012). Brand positioning statement example: Zipcar. Retrieved from http://www.brandingstrategyinsider.com/2012/04/brand-positioning-statement-example-zipcar.html.

Murrell, P. C. (2001). *The community teacher: A framework for effective urban teaching.* New York, NY: Teacher's College Press.

Norris, S. (2016). Higher attaining but emotional brittle: Why we need to assess how school marketing policies affect students. *Forum, 58*(1), 87–92.

Porter, M. (1980). *Competitive strategy: Techniques for analyzing industries and competitors*. New York, NY: Free Press.

Ries, A., & Trout, J. (1982). *Positioning: The battle for your mind*. New York, NY: Warner Books.

Robinson, C. K. (2012). Peter Drucker on marketing: Application and implications for libraries. *Managing Library Finance, 25,* 4–12.

Smiley, A. D., Howland, A. A., & Anderson, J. A. (2008). Cultural brokering as a core practice of a special education parent liaison program in a large urban school district. *Journal of Urban Learning, Teaching, and Research, 4,* 86–95.

Smith, Wendell R. (1956). Product differentiation and market segmentation as alternative marketing strategies. *Journal of Marketing, 21*(1), 3–8.

Solomon, M. (2004). *Consumer behavior: Buying, having, and being* (6th ed.). Upper Saddle River, NJ: Prentice Hall.

Turner, E. (2018). Marketing diversity: Selling school districts in a racialized marketplace. *Journal of Education Policy, 33*(6), 793–817.

UPS's Values, Mission and Strategy. (n.d.). Retrieved from https://pressroom.ups.com/pressroom/ContentDetailsViewer.page?ConceptType=FactSheets&id=1426321650156-161.

Purpose, Values & Principles. (n.d.). Retrieved from https://en-ae.pg.com/policies-and-practices/purpose-values-and-principles/.

Chapter Two

Strategic Marketing Planning

> Marketing is not bragging, and touting one's wares is not evil. The baker in the medieval town square must holler, "Fresh rolls!" if he hopes to feed the townsfolk.
>
> —Jeffrey Zeldman, Entrepreneur
> and Founder of A List Apart Webzine

The billboard on the highway outside of a large city in the Southeast US advertises a private school with the slogan "Preparing for College. Preparing for Life." The internet ads say the same thing. The secretary answers the phone with that. When you are put on hold, you hear a description of that slogan and get directed to the school's web page, which greets you with that slogan again, and there are numerous rotating pictures of students in libraries, science labs, and in front of computers—all happy, but serious. All of these images and the constant use of the phrase convey an understanding that these students are preparing for college—and for life. The phrase and advertising are ubiquitous. People who have never had children describe the school as a good place to prepare for college.

HOW DID THAT SCHOOL COME TO MARKET ITSELF LIKE THIS?

Within organizations, the marketing function plays a pivotal role. Marketing participates in the development of corporate strategies and assists in the planning, implementation, and evaluation of those strategies. The

manner in which the marketing function is structured is highly dependent
on the size and scope of the organization. For example, large corporations
with many business units will have a correspondingly large marketing
division, while the owner himself may make the marketing decisions for
a small business.

In this chapter, we will review the marketing process and discuss practical ways in which the marketing process can be incorporated into a public
school setting. The strategic marketing process can be broken out into four
distinct steps: analysis, planning, implementation, and evaluation/control
(Cravens, 1994).

MARKETING ANALYSIS AND PLANNING

Before a marketing strategy can be pursued, an analysis of the markets
to be served must first be completed. A market is defined as the set of all
actual and potential buyers of a product or service (Armstrong & Kotler,
2013). As we reviewed in Chapter 2, the marketing analysis process entails
four main steps: segmentation, target market selection, marketing strategy,
and positioning. Other aspects of the situation analysis process include
gathering marketing intelligence, which was reviewed in Chapter 4. Once
the analysis phase has been completed, the organization is ready to focus
more specifically on planning each component of the marketing mix.

As we have stated, the marketing mix includes product, price, place,
and promotion. The term was first coined in 1964 by Harvard marketing professor Neil Borden, who credited Professor James Culliton with
describing the marketing executive as a "mixer of ingredients" (Borden,
1984, p. 7). As Borden explains, the competitive and environmental circumstances facing an organization are ever changing. Management can
respond in a number of ways, including developing products, expanding
distribution outlets, changing pricing procedures, or utilizing aggressive
promotions. While these may be day-to-day responses, the overall strategy represents the organization's marketing mix.

Strategic planning for products or services encompasses three areas:
planning for new products, managing strategies for existing successful
products, and developing programs for unsuccessful products (Cravens,
1994). Organizations must put in place systems for gauging a product's

performance. Performance can be measured in both a financial and non-financial manner. Financial metrics include revenues, costs, and profit.

Nonfinancial assessments include such things as customer awareness and satisfaction measurements. From a marketing perspective, financial measurements that make sense for schools include enrollment and costs. From a nonfinancial standpoint, there are many measures a school could use to its competitive advantage—parental satisfaction survey results, test scores, college placement, and scholarship statistics, to name only a few.

Strategic planning decisions for product distribution must be consistent with the product and its positioning. A good distribution network can actually create a competitive advantage for a brand. Organizations must be able to deliver the product in a manner that meets customers' needs. Traditional businesses have a number of logistical issues to plan for, such as transportation, warehousing, inventory, and order processing. In addition, businesses must consider whether their distribution network will incorporate traditional brick-and-mortar locations, utilize a virtual e-commerce platform, or a combination of both. For schools, these same options are now available.

Where pricing is concerned, product managers must plan an effective strategy for the brand. In general, a product's price quantifies the value of the exchange. Where complex purchases are concerned, price is considered synonymous with quality (Cravens, 1994), and for some parents that is how they view the quality of schools. A company can employ any number of pricing strategies to achieve a particular objective. For example, a low-price strategy can be used to increase market share, stimulate demand, or respond to competition. Effective pricing strategies can also be used to help a company improve financial performance or establish its product positioning. Chapter 3 addresses the unique circumstances that surround "pricing decisions" for public schools.

Promotion strategy combines advertising, personal selling, sales promotion, and public relations. Often referred to as the promotion mix, these tools can dramatically influence an organization's ability to successfully influence consumer decision-making. Selection of the appropriate promotional tools must take into consideration the specific marketing objective the organization wishes to achieve. Further, because the promotional mix represents significant costs, organizations must identify the manner in which the promotional budget will be established.

Organizations typically utilize one of four methods for setting the promotional budget (Kotler & Keller, 2015). The first budgeting method uses a percentage of sales. Employed by organizations with a good sense of their sales history and reliable sales forecasting methods, this approach sets a fixed percentage of sales, such as 10 percent, to use as the marketing budget moving forward. While this method is popular with many industries, it tends to ignore sales cycles and can lead to overpromotion in periods when sales are naturally slow or underpromotion in a competitive selling environment.

The second method, competitive parity, is tied to the spending levels of competitors. However, this method ignores the differences that exist between competitors and the marketing strategies being pursued. The third approach to setting a promotional budget recognizes the financial limitations that exist in many organizations, especially small businesses. Called simply the all-you-can-afford method, the business sets aside for promotion an amount that can fit within the overall operating budget. The final method is referred to as objective and task. This method outlines communication objectives and the tasks necessary to achieve them. From there, the costs associated with each task are calculated. This approach to budgeting is the most logical and widely used method.

The marketing planning process, while detailed and time consuming, forces organizations to consider all decisions related to the marketing mix before blindly jumping in. Such forethought allows organizations to contemplate the consequences the planned marketing mix efforts will have on the organization in terms of costs, revenues, timetable, and competitive reactions, to name just a few variables. Most organizations establish annual marketing plans and update that plan quarterly to allow for adjustments based on developing challenges or opportunities. The components of a marketing plan, as recommended by the American Marketing Association, are provided in the appendix.

However, regardless of how detailed a plan the organization develops, the key components of a marketing plan include the situation analysis and the marketing plan (Lehmann & Winer, 1991). The situation analysis addresses the economic and business environment in which the organization is operating, along with the problems or opportunities currently being faced. The marketing plan outlines the strategies the organization hopes to achieve within the time period of the plan, along with the products or services that will be sold, the customers being pursued, the competition, and the specific tactics that will be undertaken—broken out by product, price, place, and promotion. The marketing plan will also include any relevant research supporting the proposed marketing plan actions, along with the key financial documentation—the marketing budget and a profit/loss statement.

For nonbusiness organizations looking to adopt a marketing orientation, the best way to begin is to appoint a marketing committee charged with identifying the problems and opportunities facing the organization (Kotler & Keller, 2015). Beyond that, the committee should consider what type of marketing function would fit within the institutional framework and whether or not there is a need for a full-time marketing manager or staff. In the next section, we will discuss ways public schools can adopt a marketing orientation.

We are making some assumptions that as a public school employee reading this book you are concerned with how to market your school better. You realize things need to change to improve your school's marketing efforts, and hopefully you have learned from the first two chapters that educational marketing is more than just telling your story. It is a whole concerted effort of research, analysis, and then implementation.

First, analysis. Determining the need for a marketing orientation for schools is a great place to start. Why are you considering this? Are other schools taking your students? Is there an upcoming bond referendum around the corner? Or do you just want to change the overall perceptions of the schools in the community? Or is there another reason underlying your motivation is very important to understand where you want to go, and will help you determine when you get there.

Analyze your situation. As asked above, are others taking students away from your schools? Is the perception your school is a "tax-wasting parasite" where nothing good happens? This can be done with some of the research mentioned in Chapter 5, but changing an established reputation of public schools should heavily involve teachers. Like the bank teller described in later parts of this chapter, teachers are the front line of relations with your parents and your community. Additionally, there are many more teachers in your community than administrators, and for most people they are the only constant contact they have with schools. They are vital, important, and often the key to your success.

Analysis is key to develop a marketing orientation. Later on we will talk about planning, implementation, and evaluation.

IMPLEMENTING YOUR MARKETING EFFORTS

An organization's overall marketing strategy guides the annual marketing planning process. Successful implementation of the plan requires the consensus and coordination of all of the organization's functional areas (Lehmann & Winer, 1991). For example, if the goal for a bank is to differentiate itself based on superior customer service, the marketing manager must recognize that the branch employees provide the service.

In order for the bank to deliver on that service promise and secure that competitive position, the marketing department will have to research customers' definition of "superior service" and communication—or possibly even train—branch workers how to deliver those key aspects of service. In other words, no amount of advertising can create that superior service brand positioning if what happens inside the bank branch does not match customers' expectations. A comprehensive marketing plan considers all aspects of the marketing mix, attending to every detail in order to ensure the overall marketing strategy is attained. This is especially important with how teachers and staff interact with parents and community members.

A marketing plan outlines the activities to be undertaken, along with the timetable and who is responsible for the implementation and how it will be executed. However, as thorough as the plan is, its effectiveness is rooted in three key factors: organizational design, incentives, and communication (Cravens, 1994).

An organization's structure can either foster or hinder the effective implementation of a marketing plan. Large, multi-unit businesses often have intricate marketing organizations due to the complex nature of the customers being served by the organization. However, an intricate marketing function is not a necessity. Organizations with flat, flexible designs can actually encourage communication between units and contribute to the successful implementation of the marketing plan.

Allocating responsibility to the individuals or units whose job it is to implement a particular aspect of the marketing plan is a challenge for many organizations. For this reason, rewards or incentives are another component of successful marketing plan implementation. We recognize the fact that public schools on the whole do not have the ability to offer employee bonuses; however, contests or basic employee recognition can go a long way toward providing the motivation necessary to gain the level of employee buy-in needed to ensure the successful implementation of the marketing plan.

Finally, communication—both horizontal and vertical—is vital to any marketing organization. In corporations, the marketing function often serves a pivotal role in collecting and disseminating information related to the implementation of the marketing plan. Methods of communication can include status reports, meetings, or informal communication designed to track how well the plan is being implemented, competitors' actions, or any other internal or external changes in the operating environment that may affect the marketing plan.

Internal and external factors can also affect the success or failure of the marketing plan's implementation (Cravens, 1994). Internally, an organization that has adopted a marketing orientation will have the greatest chance at successfully implementing the marketing plan. Put simply, this means that every function in the organization (including finance and operations) has adopted a customer-centric focus.

External consultants or suppliers can also affect the marketing plan's success. These can include advertising or PR firms, printing companies, or any other outside businesses that support the marketing plan. Because these external functions do not play a direct role in serving the organization's customers, it is important that their responsibilities be clearly defined and communicated.

As we have outlined, the successful implementation of a marketing plan is as much a function of the ideas contained in the plan as the coordination and management of the activities that support the plan—and the individuals or groups responsible for their execution.

Get everybody on board: bus drivers, coaches, secretaries, other administrators, and especially the teachers. Everybody. People form their opinions of organizations based on the personal interactions with just a few employees. Most people have no understanding of the reach and complexity of a public school, but they know the bus driver who picks up their kids or the teacher who also coaches soccer and plays "favorites" and sometimes seems rude. Or the time they came to pick up their kid from school and all the signs outside the school say visitors must report to the office, but within the school was confusion and there were no signs pointing toward the office and no one to help.

All public school employees need to understand they are representatives of the school at all times, not just at open houses and established meet-and-greets. Teachers have always been under heightened scrutiny in the US, and this has meant having high standards for employees. Here is an example from about 100 years ago. Clearly, there have been high expectations for school employees' behavior. Truly, the lifestyle of a schoolteacher has changed radically in the past 50 or 60 years. For example, a 1915 teachers' magazine listed the following rules of conduct for teachers of that day.

Rules for 1915 Schoolteachers

- You will not marry during the term of your contract.
- You are not to keep company with men.
- You must be home between the hours of 8 pm and 6 am unless attending a school function.
- You may not loiter downtown in any of the ice cream stores.
- You may not travel beyond the city limits unless you have the permission of the chairman of the board.
- You may not ride in a carriage or automobile with any man unless he is your father or brother.
- You may not smoke cigarettes.
- You may under no circumstances dye your hair.
- You may not dress in bright colors.
- You must wear at least two petticoats.
- Your dresses must not be any shorter than two inches above your ankle.
- To keep the schoolroom neat and clean, you must: scrub the floor at least once a week with hot, soapy water; clean the blackboards at least once a day; and start the fire at 7 am so the room will be warm by 8 am. (Pennsylvania State Education Association, 2013)

In the next section, we will address methods for evaluating the marketing plan.

EVALUATING THE IMPACT OF YOUR PLAN

The age-old management expression that a "mediocre strategy well executed is better than a great strategy poorly executed" (Martin, 2010) highlights the importance of measuring the marketing plan. Strategic evaluation helps ensure that performance matches objectives. There are three types of evaluation (Cravens, 1994). The first seeks to identify new opportunities or threats. The second form of evaluation looks to keep marketing performance in line with management expectations. The third form of evaluation is used to solve problems.

The marketing plan is established to achieve specific performance objectives, such as revenue, consumer awareness, or market share. Progress toward the objectives should be measured on a continuing basis. Sales-oriented organizations, for example, focus regularly on four key measures of effectiveness: sales volume, sales growth, profitability, and customer satisfaction (Cravens, Ingram, LaForge, & Young, 1992). Organizations should identify the manner in which they will collect data to be used for performance measures—either through internal sources, through other industry or subscription-based research services, or by conducting their own annual measurements, such as customer surveys.

In some cases, organizations conduct a full-blown audit of their marketing activities. The marketing audit considers not only the internal or external variables that impact the marketing plan but reviews the plan itself. The purpose is to identify gaps or deficiencies that are not being addressed by the current marketing plan or by the organization's existing marketing framework (Goetsch, 1983).

The marketing audit goes beyond standard performance measures and looks at the organization's culture in terms of its commitment to a marketing orientation and the internal systems that support the marketing effort. It also extensively examines the products and services offered by the organization, the existing market conditions and customer profile, the competitive environment, and the promotional activities that support product sales.

Whether or not an organization undertakes a marketing audit, the methods, timetable, and responsibilities for measurement should be identified by the organization prior to the implementation of the marketing plan. However, beyond collecting the information, the organization must

evaluate the data and use it to take corrective action—either to correct
weaknesses or maintain strengths. Often referred to as annual plan control
(Kotler & Keller, 2015), the evaluation process needs to be consistent and
objective, occur at regular intervals appropriate to the activities contained
in the marketing plan, and apply to all levels of the organization.

THE MARKETING PROCESS FOR PUBLIC SCHOOLS

The strategic planning process is not a new concept for public schools;
however, the introduction of strategic marketing planning is likely quite
novel. As we will discuss throughout the book, public schools, for the
most part, have enjoyed a steadily supplied customer base for the services
they provide. Recent changes to the educational landscape, including
charter schools, vouchers, and even online educational options, have
transformed the competitive environment for education—resulting in the
need for schools to more actively market themselves. Nonetheless, while
there are specific case-study examples where public schools have been
able to successfully market to their audience, the marketing planning and
implementation process is not traditionally thought of as a public school
administrator's responsibility.

Although marketing is not customarily associated with public schools,
the process is not at all unknown to private schools. Private schools have
long recognized the need for a well-organized and efficient marketing
operation. In order to give public school educators an idea of the kind of
marketing activities that their private school counterparts engage in, we
have interviewed several private school heads and marketing directors
about their strategic marketing operation. In this section, we will review
the steps in the marketing planning process by highlighting some of the
tips and suggestions offered by private P–12 school administrators, along
with private high school marketers.

Beginning with target market identification, most private schools identify anywhere from three to six separate target audiences. These include
students (and potential students), parents (and potential parents), alums,
faculty, board members, and the community at-large. The structure of
the marketing team is often designed to support these target audiences.
Positions include a communications or marketing director, along with

an admissions staff, and alumni relations and/or development staff. In most cases, the marketing/communications team also includes the head of school and individuals who actively participate in the marketing planning process, as well as contribute to and review the messages that are a part of the communications process.

The planning process for private schools takes several different forms. Most private schools have a long-range, 5- or 10-year plan, addressing the long-term vision for the growth and development of the school. The marketing function is an important component of the long-range plan. However, these schools also develop annual marketing plans that will help them achieve their specific performance goals in admissions or development, for example. In one Midwestern P–12 school, the planning process begins over the summer. Here, major marketing goals and communication themes are mapped out for the coming year. In addition, the methods by which these themes will be communicated are also reviewed in much the same way that a magazine outlines an annual editorial agenda.

Most private schools have a number of different communications vehicles, ranging from quarterly or semiannual printed magazines that are mailed out to every stakeholder group, to monthly or weekly online blogs or newsletters directed to parents, faculty, and board members, to weekly letters from school division heads (early childhood, elementary school, middle school, and high school) emailed to families. In fact, one school communications director noted that the shift to electronic forms of communication has not only allowed the school to reduce its marketing costs for printing but increase its timeliness and turnaround.

While there are many marketing objectives outlined by private schools, the foremost objective is admissions. With that in mind, the marketing activities are structured to support the admissions cycle. Open houses, tours, parent breakfasts or coffees, student shadow dates, and admissions test dates are among the event-focused activities designed to attract families to schools.

As one Midwestern college preparatory high school noted, the goal is to get people in the building so they can experience the culture and visualize the experience. Time spent on campus is especially important for prospective middle and high school students. These schools understand that a significant portion of a student's waking day is spent at school. For early childhood and elementary schools, both the parents and the child must be comfortable in the environment. Private schools appreciate that a school decision is emotional as much as it is logical.

Well-designed collateral materials and websites further support the school's marketing effort. Beyond the communications magazines and newsletters, schools have admissions and fund-raising materials reinforcing the positioning of the school. Private schools understand their operating environment extremely well and do an effective job of differentiating themselves from their competitors. Mission statements and philosophies are clearly communicated in positioning slogans, learning pillars, hallmarks, or core values. Below are examples of how private schools use these themes to readily communicate their distinguishing characteristics.

Sample Positioning Slogans

Celebrating 200 Years
Engaged in Learning. Engaged in Life.
Experience the Difference
Knowledge and Values for a Lifetime

Sample Core Values/Hallmarks/Pillars

Caring
Challenging
Civic responsibility
Classic curriculum
Compassion
Connected
Constructive
Constructivist
Critical thinking
Developmental
Differentiated
Engaged
Ethical judgment and action
Excellence
Faith
Global

Global citizenship and cultural
  competence
Global readiness
Impactful
Inclusive
Innovative
Integrity
Inviting
Involved
Leadership
Participatory
Personal discipline
Relational
Relevant
Respect
Respectful

Responsibility

Rigorous

Service

Small by design

Students are known

Successful

Supportive

Traditional

Transformative

United

Visionary

As can be seen, these are more than just advertising headlines. The pillars and hallmarks represent the core product (service) being sold to customers and delivered to students. They are at the heart of the school's value exchange. These schools consistently communicate the differentiating features of their programs in their marketing materials. More importantly, these themes serve as the distinguishing features of the educational product and give prospective families and students a sense of the intangible benefits being offered by the school.

In terms of the budgetary planning to support the marketing program, anywhere from 2 to 5 percent of a school's operating budget is devoted to marketing/admissions/alumni relations and development. Chapter 6 will discuss in greater detail some of the specific promotional activities schools implement to help achieve their marketing objectives. However, many schools use specific metrics to identify whether or not their implementation efforts are on pace to meet the performance objective. For example, where admissions are concerned, schools will track traffic patterns, such as attendance at open houses and number of scheduled shadow visits, in order to ensure they are on pace to meet their application and admissions goals.

Where private schools excel in the strategic marketing process is with evaluation. Private schools take the time to collect formal and informal feedback from their various constituencies. They use the responses not only to inform future marketing planning but also to identify the perceived strengths and weaknesses of their overall operation so they can address issues accordingly. Some schools participate in formal, industry-sponsored surveys. For example, the Independent Schools Association of the Central States (ISACS) offers member schools the opportunity to participate in surveys they conduct.

The results not only provide participating schools with valuable feedback on their own performance but also allow for benchmark comparisons to other private schools. However, many schools collect their own data, using formal quantitative surveys, along with a variety of qualitative methods, such as parent conversations and student focus groups. For example, one school had students in a rhetoric class examine its admission materials. The valuable feedback alerted the marketing team to subtle themes and underlying messages that students keenly perceive.

In one instance, students noted that a picture showing a student talking on a cell phone was already outdated—in a brochure that was only two years old. Not only was the phone technology outmoded, but also students today are more likely to text, rather than speak on the phone. The school's communication director noted that adults would be less apt to pick up on that image but recognized the importance of the observation, noting that the school didn't want its image to be viewed as old or dated. As a result, the school makes it a point to minimize photographic depictions of personal technology or other quickly dated fads in its marketing materials. Using both quantitative and qualitative data allows schools to make changes to the marketing mix and better meet the needs of their target customers.

The strategic marketing process allows organizations to effectively plan a marketing program that considers all 4*P*s. While many public school districts have public information and communications officers, that role is only one aspect of the marketing function—promotion. We advocate for the adoption of the marketing concept by public schools, one that comprehensively integrates all aspects of product, price, place, and promotion to the value exchange. Peter Drucker has a great quote regarding marketing: "Marketing is so basic that it cannot be considered a separate function within the business . . . But it is, first, a central dimension of the entire business."

What separates marketing organizations from all others is the manner in which marketing is viewed. Organizations who do not uphold an integrated marketing concept look upon "marketing" solely as communications. Furthermore, they view that role as an afterthought. For example, they design products and programs first—and then try to figure out where and how to "market" them. Conversely, marketing organizations consider the consumers' needs up front and embrace the strategic marketing planning process as a way to ensure that those needs will be considered through every aspect of the value chain.

CASE STUDY:
Colonial Grove Strategic Planning Process

Colonial Grove (CG) is a small, independent private school offering pre-school through high school on one small campus. They prefer to evaluate themselves on what type of individuals they create, rather than a state imposed standard of measurement. They do not strive to be the biggest. They have found their student population "sweet spot" to be between 950 and 1,000. In many ways their goal is not to grow or be the best school for everyone, but they do want to "skim the cream from the top of the milk."

They use national metrics and watch other schools around the globe, rather than paying close attention to local politics and competitors. In meetings with school leaders, you hear them talking about education in very family-friendly terms. Ways that people in the community, who may not have a professional background in education, would understand and respond well to. While they are an elite educational experience with countless attributes, they are fabulously approachable and accessible to the untrained eye.

It is not surprising that when it came time for them to become engaged in a new strategic planning process that they broached it in a very trans-parent and collaborative way. They created a visual representation of their efforts, established a robust steering committee representing various backgrounds and levels of involvement, set an ambitious timeline for a final presentation to their board of directors, and also set three strategic focus areas for their work: Teaching and Learning, Citizenship and Com-munity, and Sustainability and Stewardship. Additionally, they followed a three-phase process to keep their efforts focused and moving forward.

Phase 1: Learning Phase

The first phase consisted of approximately three months of data collec-tion. This involved talking with lots of people in the community, espe-cially people who had no connection to their school. They wanted to know what people outside of the CG experience thought about their school. They specifically sought to find out how they were perceived by others. They also did comprehensive demographic analysis to find out who would be likely to choose them and how far away families would drive to attend their school.

Phase 2: Distillation Phase

The second phase of the strategic planning process included data analysis and member checking. They made sure all of the data they collected was accurate and then began to piece together what they learned in a meaningful way using their visual representation, steering committee, and three focus areas as their guides.

Phase 3: Document Creation Phase

The third phase of the process involved working on action items and creating documentation of their next steps. They created documents and a plan, which they presented to the board of directors and kicked off in the fall of the next school year.

REFERENCES

Armstrong, G., & Kotler, P. (2013). *Marketing: An introduction* (11th ed.). Boston, MA: Pearson.

Borden, N. (1984). The concept of the marketing mix. *Journal of Advertising Research, 24*(4), 7–12.

Cravens, D. (1994). *Strategic marketing* (4th ed.). Boston, MA: Irwin.

Cravens, D., Ingram, T., LaForge, R., & Young, C. (1992). Hallmarks of effective sales organizations. *Marketing Management,* Winter, 59.

Goetsch, H. (1983). Conduct a comprehensive marketing audit to improve marketing planning. *Marketing News* (March) 14. Retrieved from http://www.marketingpower.com/ResourceLibrary/Publications/MarketingNews/1983/17/6/19052581.pdf.

Kotler, P., & Keller, K. L. (2015). *Marketing management* (15th ed.). Upper Saddle River, NJ: Pearson.

Lee, L., & Hayes, D. (2007). Creating a marketing plan. Retrieved from http://www.marketingpower.com/ResourceLibrary/Pages/Best%20Practices/Creating_a Marketing_Plan.aspx.

Lehmann, D., & Winer, R. (1991). *Analysis for marketing planning* (2nd ed.). Homewood, IL: Richard D. Irwin.

Martin, R. (2010). The execution trap. Harvard Business Review. Retrieved from http://hbr.org/2010/07/the-execution-trap/ar/1\.

Pennsylvania State Education Association. (2013). Rules for teachers 1915. Retrieved from http://oldtowncoldspring.tripod.com/school1.html.

Chapter Three

The Marketing Mix Introduced: Product, Price, and Place

A good company offers excellent products and services. A great company also offers excellent products and services but also strives to make the world a better place.

—Philip Kotler, Author and Professor of Marketing at the Kellogg School of Management, Northwestern University

At the core of any leader's understanding of marketing should be a foundational appreciation for the marketing mix, often referred to as the 4Ps—product, price, place, and promotion. These four components come together to create the value proposition offered to the consumer. Accordingly, they need to complement one another to support the product's positioning. For example, consumers would expect that a high-end product, such as an automobile, will be distinctive, responsive, and equipped with the foremost design and performance features. Likewise, the automobile would be sold at a higher price. In terms of distribution, to sell such a car on a corner lot with a flashing neon sign reading, "Buy here. Pay here," would not be consistent with the brand identity. Rather, the place where such a car is sold should be a well-appointed showroom with salespeople who are knowledgeable, well dressed, and professional. Finally, the promotion of the vehicle should not feature direct mail coupons for discounts. Instead, a television commercial showing the car being driven along a curving road or parked in front of an elegant country estate is more fitting.

This chapter provides details on how organizations build a marketing mix, along with the management considerations for each component.

PRODUCT

The product is the thing of value that is at the heart of the value exchange. It is the good or service for which consumers are willing to exchange something of value in return. Within this framework, we will evaluate public school education as a product and discuss the unique operating and competitive characteristics affecting the industry.

To begin, we should distinguish that within the marketing mix, the term *product* is used to represent both products and services. Products are defined as anything offered for use or consumption to satisfy a need or want (Armstrong & Kotler, 2013). Products are physical, tangible goods that can be classified in terms of consumer products and industrial products. Consumer products can be classified based on the level of purchasing effort consumers expend in order to attain them (Murphy & Enis, 1986). They include:

- Convenience products: Items that are frequently purchased and with minimal shopping effort.
- Shopping products: Items that are purchased occasionally and for which the consumer is willing to expend some effort to compare options, based on styling, price, or quality.
- Specialty products: Items that are infrequently purchased and for which consumers make an extensive purchasing effort.
- Unsought products: Items the consumer does not normally think about purchasing and that require considerable promotion in order to get them to consider for purchase.

The industrial products classification group items are purchased by organizations for a variety of purposes. These include raw materials and parts, capital items, and supplies and services.

A service is defined as any act or performance one party can offer to another that is essentially intangible and does not result in the ownership of anything (Kotler & Keller, 2012). Services are the fastest growing component of the world's economy, comprising nearly two-thirds of the gross world product ("GDP and the Economy," 2011). Because of the intangible nature of services, organizations must carefully consider four important characteristics when planning and managing a service business:

- Intangibility: Refers to the elusive, untouchable nature of products; as such, they cannot be experienced prior to purchase.
- Inseparability: Signifies that the service cannot be separated from the service provider.
- Variability: Recognizes that the quality of the service delivered depends greatly on the experience and expertise of the service provider.
- Perishability: Underscores the fact that, unlike physical products, services cannot be inventoried.

In addition, because service quality is variable, it is difficult for consumers to judge them. Further, due to the intangible nature of a service, consumers can only truly evaluate them after the purchase (Ostrom & Iacobucci, 1995). Some services are high in experience qualities, such as amusement parks and haircuts, while others are high in credence qualities, like medical or legal services and automotive repair. Credence quality services are the most difficult for consumers to evaluate after the purchase. For example, a client may be determine that he was kindly or respectfully treated by a lawyer and received a reasonable resolution to the matter at hand. However, the client is not necessarily in the position to evaluate whether or not the service provided was the best possible.

Because services are typically delivered by people, service-oriented businesses focus on maximizing the relationship between both the employee and the consumer. The service profit chain is the term used to describe the link between the employee's effort and the customer's satisfaction (Yee, Yeung, & Cheng, 2011). The links in the service profit chain include:

- Internal service quality: Superior employee selection and training, a positive work environment, and effective customer-service systems. This results in . . .
- Satisfied and productive service employees. This results in . . .
- Greater service value: Effective and efficient service delivery. This results in . . .
- Satisfied and loyal customers who are loyal, make repeat purchases, and refer other customers. This results in . . .
- Healthy services profits and organizational growth, which can be considered characteristics of a superior service firm.

THE PRODUCT LIFE CYCLE AND THE
IMPLICATIONS FOR EDUCATION

The product life cycle concept is based on the fact that "a product's sales volume follows a typical four-phase cycle" (Clifford, 1965, p. 34). The states in the product life cycle include:

- Introduction: The product is new to the marketplace. Sales are slow, and heavy promotion is used to create awareness.
- Growth: Sales begin to increase, and other competitors enter the market. Promotional efforts shift to reinforcing product positioning against growing competition.
- Maturity: The product concept is widely recognized, sales pace begins to slow, no new competitors enter the market, and some competitors may drop out.
- Decline: Sales decrease at an increasing pace. The product's usefulness may have been usurped by other products or innovations. The product is either removed from the market or repositioned for new uses or audiences.

To apply this concept to education, we must first state that our intention is not to advocate for or against competition in education. Nor can we, in the scope of this book, cover the full impact of competition on the field. We are, however, discussing how public schools should begin to navigate the new competitive waters within which they find themselves and incorporate effective marketing strategies into their current practices.

Educators should begin by utilizing the four characteristics of planning and managing a service business. From an educator's perspective the four characteristics (intangibility, inseparability, variability, and perishability) of planning and managing a service business could be interpreted as follows:

- Intangibility: Educational experience of students attending your school. Public schools have a long history of providing high-quality education for the masses. The large majority of the populace develops a perspective on schools based on publicized test scores. In most cases, families and students believe that the educational experience received from their public school is good, while the experiences and levels of quality of all other public schools are bad. Very few families and community members take the time to visit schools their children do not attend. It is very important for public schools to provide the appropriate variety of information to the community so that the community as a whole has a notion of what the educational experience in the building is like.

- Inseparability: Remembering that the service cannot be distinguished from the service provider(s), schools have the opportunity to showcase their superiority through their staff. Unfortunately, the reverse is also true, which is why we stated that so much of how parents evaluate the school is based on the one-on-one interactions they have with school leaders, faculty, and staff members.
- Variability: Quality can vary from one service provider to the other. Thus, having one or two outstanding teachers does not mean that the quality of the entire school is excellent.
- Perishability: Services cannot be stockpiled, which means that empty schools represent lost income. In most state funding formulas, the end result is that each student represents state and federal dollars. Regardless of enrollment levels, empty rooms and buildings must still be maintained and secured, even if they are used very little. Once the final student counts are into the state, any empty seat denotes lost income for that year, which can never be recovered. Every student lost to a competitor represents lost income to the school that can never be recouped.

In addition to the four characteristics of planning and managing a service business, administrators should also consider the links in their profit chain. To work proactively as a service business, schools must examine the links in their service profit chain (Yee, Yeung, & Cheng, 2011). For schools, aligned service chain links are as follows:

- Internal service quality: Hiring highly qualified staff, teachers, and administrators and providing timely and research-based professional development and effective family engagement processes. This results in . . .
- Satisfied, productive, and dedicated staff, teachers, and administrators. This results in . . .
- Greater service value: Effective and efficient classrooms, extracurricular activities, interactions with families. This results in . . .
- Satisfied and loyal customers: Communities where families and community members are loyal to the school, support the school in times of

need, attend school events, recommend the school to others, and send all of their children to the school. This results in . . .
• Healthy service profits and organizational growth: Highly functioning schools that have healthy student achievement; popular extracurricular activities; satisfied staff, teachers, and administrators; and involved alumni, as well as engaged families and communities.

Unlike many businesses, public schools have a unique situation to navigate. Public schools must adhere to both state and federal mandates that, in many cases, are not fully funded. In many ways, the hands of public school leaders are tied when it comes to cutting costs because many monetary funds are restricted for designated projects. This means that, while a school may have a $10 million budget, it cannot make arbitrary decisions about how to spend or save those dollars. In other business models, administrators have full authority to utilize resources in a manner they deem most beneficial to the health of the organization.

Public education is currently in the third stage of the product life cycle. The third stage is maturity. Public education is facing the following realities:

• Sales growth slows: The number of students who are choosing public education is decreasing at an increasing rate. The number of students who are choosing a nonpublic education is increasing.
• Product concept is widely accepted: Public education, in many ways, has been around since the postindustrial era with very few changes. A large majority of the population is familiar with and/or has utilized public education.
• No new competitors entering the market: In natural market conditions, the market share is fixed. Given new legislation and policy (vouchers and charters), traditional public education is not facing a natural market in maturity.
• Sales growth to new customers is difficult: Public schools are struggling to keep current students and recruit students away from private education.

The importance of the third point cannot be overstated. The impact of unnatural market factors (new competitors) during a fixed time is crucial. The market for public education is shrinking based on population growth, yet more schools are being added to an already saturated marketplace.

This only increases the stakes for public schools and pushes the cycle toward the decline phase. In times like this, public schools must focus on the five guidelines that direct decision-making during this time of financial uncertainty:

- Increase investments
- Get closer to customers
- Review budget allocations
- Focus on the most compelling value proposition
- Evaluate the brand and product offerings

PRICE

In most cases, price is at the heart of the value exchange. It quantifies the value that the consumer must give up in order to acquire the item of value they desire in return. For an organization, pricing strategy is extremely important, as it is the only element in the marketing mix that generates revenue. Pricing strategy is complex and involves not only an intricate understanding of the firm's production costs and its revenue goals, but a solid grasp on a variety of external economic factors, including competition and demand, as well as behavioral variables such as consumer perception.

Most organizations consider a variety of pricing strategies and engage in extensive analysis to forecast the impact on sales of different pricing models. Given that public education is not tuition based, this book will not engage in a lengthy discussion of pricing strategies. Rather, we will provide a basic framework of pricing strategies and use this framework as a guide to discuss how consumers interpret price as a measure of value.

Pricing strategy is a function of the product's position, as well as its stage in the product life cycle. Organizations will carefully forecast the movement in price as a product moves through the cycle. Figure 3.1 demonstrates options for pricing of new products.

Products that utilize price skimming set a high initial price as a means of skimming as much revenue as possible from each layer of the market (Armstrong & Kotler, 2013). Firms set an initial high price when the product is introduced and is perceived to have unique advantages. This strategy generally works only when consumers are willing to buy the product

Figure 3.1. **New Product Pricing Strategies**

even though it carries an above-average price tag. As the firm enters the growth and maturity stages of the life cycle, when competition increases, the price is generally lowered.

At the other end of the continuum is penetration pricing. Firms pursuing this strategy set a low price as a way to reach out to a mass market. This strategy is designed to capture large market shares, which will contribute to lower production costs as a result of the firm realizing economies of scale. Penetration pricing is typically utilized by products with few, if any, unique points of differentiation. Unlike price skimming, which encourages competition, the low price point utilized in penetration pricing typically discourages competition.

Other firms try to avoid pricing wars by simply setting prices in line with competition. Also referred to as going rate pricing, status quo pricing is simple to implement, though it tends to ignore demand or production costs. Typically, this strategy is employed in competitive marketplaces.

Once the base price for a product is established, a firm will implement any number of price adjustment strategies to react to the competitive environment. Options range from discounts and promotional pricing to geographic and psychological pricing.

As Warren Buffet stated, "Price is what you pay. Value is what you get." This quote gets to the root of marketing—the value exchange. However, as we have stated, in most cases, the consumer is giving up something of value—typically money—to receive something of value in return—a haircut or a new pair of shoes, for example.

On the most basic level, the value exchange for public education is quite similar. Parents pay taxes to support a public school system in exchange for which they have the opportunity to have their children receive an education. However, families alone do not fund the purchase; rather, the community at large supports the educational system through their taxes. The value delivered by public schools should be understood by every stakeholder group the school serves—and it is the school's responsibility to make it known.

Although there is no price point being charged for public education, the value proposition allows schools to convey the degree of the value exchange to the intended target market. For example, a charter school that emphasizes a math and science curriculum will identify a very narrow target of families wishing to stress those subjects in their children's educations. To the extent that such a curriculum is perceived as so unique and different, consumers may be attracted to the school in the same way that some consumers are easily attracted to revolutionary new products, thereby allowing the school to skim away students from other schools in much the same way as novel products employ a price skimming tactic when they enter the market.

Again, because the consumer is not paying tuition for public education, it is difficult to make exact parallels to the pricing strategies used by other products and services. For example, schools that target a mass volume of students and wish to convey the sense of having something for everyone could be likened to a penetration strategy, which emphasizes large volume. However, while a penetration pricing strategy can easily work for many mass-marketed goods, we caution schools against conveying a mass appeal value message. As we have stated previously, the pricing models and techniques employed by private industry do not apply to a public industry product like education. Nonetheless, we do hold tightly to the notion that the lack of a price tag does not mean that no value is being exchanged. On the contrary, public schools deliver tremendous value in exchange for many things, such as the time, effort, and interest of students and parents, as well as the tax support, goodwill, and feeling of pride from the community in which the school operates.

PLACE

As any good retailer knows, where a business is located is extremely important. Location, location, location. Traditional businesses plan a product placement strategy that will help them deliver products to their customers faster and more efficiently. With this in mind, we introduce another member of the value chain: the marketing intermediary. This can include wholesalers, distributors, and retailers, all of whom help sellers broaden their distribution capabilities. As we will demonstrate, the middleman—whose name is often spoken with disdain—actually provides efficiencies. In reality, consumers do not go from one manufacturer to purchase shoes and then to another to buy pants. Rather, manufacturers utilize sophisticated logistical systems to send their products through the value chain to retailers who are more conveniently located near the consumer and who sell other items the consumer may also need or want.

Simply put, marketing channels "can be viewed as sets of interdependent organizations involved in the process of making a product or service available for use or consumption (Stern & El-Ansary, 1982, p. 3). These include indirect and direct options. Indirect options utilize marketing intermediaries with multiple channels, such as wholesalers and retailers. Others utilize a single channel, sending the product directly from the manufacturer to the retailer, who then sells it to the end user.

The direct marketing option is also referred to as a zero channel, where the product is delivered directly from the seller to the buyer. Many products are distributed through direct marketing methods, which utilize a variety of promotional means, including catalogs and websites. Education, either in its traditional in-school or online format, is delivered via direct channels. In this chapter, we will discuss the channels of distribution for public schools.

The value chain for public education is the string of groups that work together to provide society with an educated populace. For public schools, the value chain is quite simple given that it delivers a product via a direct channel. The educational value chain starts with families and communities sending their children to the public schools. Then, public schools provide students with an education and send them to college or some type of postsecondary educational setting. Educational institutions produce alumni who will be taxpayers and voters and then become the families and communities that send their children to public schools, and the chain starts over again (Figure 3.2).

In many cases, the simplicity of this model has led many public schools to employ someone to handle communications or public relations. Unfortunately, this has proven for many public schools to be too little too late.

Figure 3.2. **External Educational Value Chain**

This big-picture perspective on education as a product is important to keep in mind but is not the only piece of the story. Given that education is a service, it is also important to define an internal value chain through the lens of service to adequately address the needs of public schools.

According to the *Harvard Business Review* (Martin, 2010), top service agencies recognize the direct correlation between employee satisfaction and customer satisfaction. From an internal perspective, the importance of employee satisfaction cannot be overstated. For public schools, this means staff members who work directly with students, and families have the greatest opportunity to make an impact on achievement, retention, and recruitment. Public schools have a long history of understanding the important role staff plays in student achievement, but in the era of school choice this is not enough. Public schools must be conscious of retention and recruitment. The educational value chain is shown in Figure 3.3:

Each link in the educational value chain is critical to the health of a public school. A high-quality experience for staff would include physical work environment, professional development opportunities, supplies and technology for working with students, and recognition programs.

All of these things are vital to ensuring a satisfied staff. With a satisfied staff, public schools are able to more accurately ensure students are receiving a high-quality experience. Families and communities are satisfied with public schools when they provide an educational experience meeting their needs. If families and the larger community are satisfied with the public education offered in their community, they will support the school in times of need. This show of support could be by voting yes to approve levees and/or referendums or could come in the form of sending additional students to the school, as well as referring the public school to other families who are school shopping. Growth of public schools is the result of family and community loyalty. This loyalty is the result of satisfaction with the value of the educational services the public school provides.

High Quality Experience for Staff → Staff Satisfaction → Staff Retention and Productivity → High Quality Experience for Students → Family and Community Satisfaction → Family and Community Loyalty → Increased Student Achievement, Retention, and Recruitment

Figure 3.3. Internal Educational Value Chain

CASE STUDY:
ESSA and Comprehensive Needs Assessments

One of the most influential shifts from the No Child Left Behind (NCLB) legislation to the Every Student Succeeds Act (ESSA) is the move from data based to evidence based. Where NCLB required schools to use data, ESSA goes a step further to require the use of evidence. ESSA even provides definitions for the levels of evidence that are acceptable. ESSA's definition of "evidence based" includes four levels of evidence. Together, they create a framework to develop an increasingly rigorous evidence base. Levels 1–3 require findings of a statistically significant effect on improving student outcomes based on the following:

(Level 1) Strong: At least 1 well-designed and well implemented *experimental study*

(Level 2) Moderate: At least 1 well-designed and well implemented *quasi-experimental study*

(Level 3) Promising: At least 1 well-designed and well implemented *correlational study* with statistical controls for selection bias

(Level 4) Under Evaluation: *Demonstrates a rationale* based on high-quality research or positive evaluation that such activity, strategy, or intervention is likely to improve student outcomes and includes *ongoing efforts to examine the effects* of such activity, strategy, or intervention

In addition to providing clear guidance on the definition of evidence based, ESSA also pushes schools to analyze their own data and match these data with evidence-based approaches. ESSA now *requires* schools to conduct comprehensive needs assessments (CNAs) in order to complete their federal- and state-level grant allocations, as well as their school improvement plans. A school or district must use data to identify strengths and challenges, determine the root causes leading to the challenges, and plan for future action. ESSA provides specific guidance to conducting CNAs.

To ensure that a school's comprehensive plan best serves the needs of those children who are failing or are at risk of failing to meet the challenging state academic standards, the school must conduct a comprehensive needs assessment (ESEA section 1114(b)(6)). Through the needs assessment, a school must consult with a broad range of stakeholders, including parents, school staff, and others in the community, and examine relevant academic achievement data to understand students' most pressing needs and their root causes (ESEA section 1114(b)(2); 34 C.F.R. § 200.26(a)). Where necessary, a school should attempt to engage in interviews, focus groups, or surveys, as well as review data on students, educators, and schools to gain a better understanding of the root causes of the identified needs.

While ESSA does allow schools more flexibility than NCLB, it requires schools to be more savvy and strategic with data and evidence. Schools must now be able to use data to describe their needs and make recommendations. As schools become more sophisticated in their grant writing, they must specifically hone their skills in writing CNAs. The following are pieces of data that should be collected as part of a CNA:

- Student performance data
- Staff input
- Leadership input
- Board member feedback
- Family feedback

These pieces of data should then be analyzed and correlated with high-quality programming that meets ESSA evidence-based requirements. In addition to the results of the CNA, most states are also requiring that schools provide a literature review on the curriculum chosen in order to show a direct match between the ability of the chosen program to address the specific needs outlined in the CNA.

REFERENCES

Armstrong, G., & Kotler, P. (2013). *Marketing: An introduction* (11th ed.). Boston, MA: Pearson.

Clifford, D. Jr. (1965). Managing the product life cycle. *Management Review, 54*(6), 34–38.

GDP and the Economy. (2011). U.S. Bureau of Economic Analysis. Retrieved from www.bea.gov/scb/pdf/2011/02%20.

Kotler, P., & Keller, K. (2012). *Marketing management* (14th ed.). Boston, MA: Prentice Hall.

Martin, R. (2010). The execution trap. *Harvard Business Review*. Retrieved from http://hbr.org/2010/07/the-execution-trap/ar/1.

Murphy, P., & Enis, B. (1986). Classifying products strategically. *Journal of Marketing, 50*(July), 24–42.

Ostrom, A., & Iacobucci, D. (1995). Consumer trade-offs and the evaluation of services. *Journal of Marketing, 59,* 17–28.

Stern, L. & El-Ansary, A. (1982). *Marketing Channels* (2nd ed.). Englewood Cliffs, NJ: Prentice-Hall.

Yee, R., Yeung, A. & Cheng, T. (2011). The service-profit chain: An empirical analysis in high-contact service industries. *International Journal of Production Economics, 130*(2), 236–245.

Chapter Four

The Marketing Mix: Promotion

Good marketing makes the company look smart. Great marketing makes the customer feel smart.

—Joe Chernov, Marketer and Former VP of Marketing at HubSpot

The final *P* of the marketing mix—promotion—is undoubtedly the aspect of the marketing mix with which consumers are most familiar. Promotion includes the various means through which the organization attempts to "inform, persuade, and remind consumers—directly or indirectly—about the products and brands they sell" (Kotler & Keller, 2012). Also referred to as the promotion mix, this aspect of the marketing mix includes its own set of tools, including advertising, public relations, personal selling, sales promotion, and direct marketing. In this chapter, we will review the components of the promotion mix and how organizations use these communication tools to help achieve their marketing objectives. First, we will briefly review the cultural and technological changes that have resulted in a shift in the manner in which organizations implement their marketing communications strategies.

Prior to the evolution of the internet and the digital age, the flow of communication from organizations to their customers was predominantly one directional. To use a simplified description of the communications process, a company would develop a message and send it through a selected media channel to the receiver, who interprets the message. However, the standard communication process, as outlined here, also allows for opportunities for feedback from the receiver to the message sender. For example, in the case of direct, face-to-face communication, the receiver can provide immediate verbal and visual feedback. However, when indirect communication, such as advertising, is employed, the receiver cannot provide direct, immediate feedback to the message sender. In other words, if a consumer does not understand the content of an advertiser's commercial, the company has no way of collecting that immediate feedback.

With the evolution of the internet and social media, the communication landscape has shifted to a model that now permits the full participation of consumers in dialogue related to companies and brands. These technologies not only enable consumers to be better informed but also facilitate the exchange of information with companies and—perhaps more importantly—with other consumers. Social media, blogs, and websites afford consumers tremendous resources to share information about their product experiences.

Technology has also impacted the messaging strategies organizations are using to promote their products. Sophisticated databases and the ability to track online behavior have given marketers the tools to move their messaging strategy from single-message broadcasting to customized-message narrowcasting (Armstrong & Kotler, 2013). In addition, marketers are joining consumers online, creating brand affinity communities on social networks and even utilizing other consumers to help create and share messages. In the latter strategy, referred to as buzz marketing, organizations enlist influential consumers or other opinion leaders to serve as ambassadors for the product; these envoys help spread the brand message using their own words and opinions. The goal of this persuasive form of communication is to increase both awareness of and affinity for the brand.

As a result of the increased technology and consumer involvement, marketers have shifted their emphasis on mass communication and have begun to look at the overall impact all of their promotional tools have on consumers. For example, a product advertising message may state one thing, a website or direct mail promotion may say something else, and an in-store salesperson may convey yet another impression. In response, marketers have moved to develop a more unified approach to their marketing communication planning process. Integrated marketing communication seeks to track all of the points where consumers may come into contact with a company and all its brands and messages for the purpose of delivering an overall streamlined, consistent message and creating a positive image for the organization. To do this, the organization must have a solid understanding of the strengths and weaknesses of each tool in the promotion mix, as well as the media channels through which marketing messages can be sent. In the next sections, we will address the various aspects of the promotion mix.

ADVERTISING

Advertising helps an organization communicate the value proposition. Advertising can be defined as the development and dissemination of messages by any sponsoring organization or individual, designed to inform or persuade a target audience about a particular product, service, or idea. The key is to understand the sender of the message has decision control over both the message content and the media selected to convey the message.

As a promotional tool, advertising offers both strengths and weaknesses. For the advertiser, advertising allows a single brand message to be conveyed to numerous consumers at once. Depending on the medium selected, advertisers can employ any number of creative techniques to communicate the message. However, because consumers recognize the advertiser is in control of the message, there is often some skepticism among buyers relative to the reliability of the claims being made in an ad. Further, due to the fact that most mass mediums reach a large audience—combined with the fact that advertising airtime or space is priced based on the size of the audience delivered—advertising, as a promotional tool, is generally very expensive.

Because paid advertising consists not only of the message content but also media selection, it is important for marketers to have a good understanding of the effective value of various forms of media. Table 4.1 provides a brief overview of the strengths and weaknesses of various forms of media.

Selecting the appropriate media for use in an advertising campaign is equally important to the proper development of the message itself. The media plan needs to consider the objective of the advertising campaign, the target audience and their media habits, the creative messaging strategy, and the budget.

Table 4.1. Media Strengths and Weaknesses

Media	Strengths	Weaknesses
Television	High reach—delivers large audiences Low cost per impression High intrusion value and credibility Numerous creative messaging options and production techniques Audience segmentation options available through varied programs	Clutter—from total number of advertisers Low recall Increased competition Channel surfing, DVR usage—means ads could be overlooked Short exposure time (typically 30 seconds) Due to large audience reached, large budgets required
Radio	Easily targeted audience due to station format Creative flexibility and low cost Delivers local audience Mobile medium	Short exposure time (typically 60 seconds) Low attention levels Increased competition from other audio sources
Outdoor	Geographic targeting Accessible for local ads High reach Low cost per impression High frequency on major commuter routes Creative flexibility	Short exposure time Creative limitations Little audience segmentation possible
Magazines	Easily targeted audience due to editorial format High color quality Long shelf life Longer attention to ad Credible Tangible	Declining readership High level of clutter Long lead time to ad showing Little flexibility High cost
Newspaper	Local audience delivery High flexibility Credible Tangible Longer message possible Coupons or inserts possible	Short shelf life Clutter from total number of advertisers Poor production quality Declining readership
Digital	Creative possibilities Short lead time to send ad Simplicity of target segmentation High audience interest Excellent measurement metrics Numerous options—search, display, mobile, games, social, banner ads	Clutter from other advertisers Difficult ad buying procedures Short life span Low intrusion value

Calder, 2008; Clow & Baack, 2001

PUBLIC RELATIONS

The Public Relations Society of America (PRSA) defines *public relations* (PR) as "a strategic communication process that builds mutually beneficial relationships between organizations and their publics" (n.d.). An organization's publics—sometimes referred to as stakeholders—includes internal and external groups. A stakeholder is an individual or group with a vested interest in the organization (Baack, 1997). Table 4.2 identifies different types of stakeholder groups.

Public relations seeks to generate interest in or awareness of the organization and its products, events, or issues. However, unlike advertising, PR seeks to cultivate this attention without paying for airtime or space. To do this, PR professionals serve a variety of functions in order to maintain positive relationships with stakeholder groups; these include the following (Armstrong & Kotler, 2013):

- Media relations: The activities involved in working with the media to generate publicity for a product, service, or organization. This includes establishing contact with media reporters, providing publicity materials to media or other groups, and being available to answer any questions the media might have.
- Product publicity: The nonpaid for communication of information about the company or product, generally in some media format. This could include product placement in television or movies.
- Public affairs: The managerial function concerned with the relationships that exist between the organization and its external environment.

Table 4.2. Types of Stakeholder Groups

Internal Stakeholders	External Stakeholders
Employees	Channel members
Volunteers	Customers
Unions	Local community
Shareholders/taxpayers	Financial community
Board members	Government
Retirees	Community organizations
Donors	Special-interest groups
Students	Media

Key tasks include intelligence gathering and analysis, internal communication, and any external initiatives directed at government, communities, or the general public.

- Lobbying: A person or group of persons seeking to influence the proceedings or efforts of legislative bodies through personal intervention.
- Investor relations: Relationships built with company stockholders or investors, as well as other representatives who work in the financial community.
- Development: Efforts by nonprofits to build relationships with donors or other stakeholders to gain financial or volunteer support.

A solid public relations strategy can be an effective part of the overall marketing plan because it can be used to address the specific needs or concerns of a narrow audience or public (as in the case of employee relations) or be a cost-effective, expedient, and credible method for reaching out to a broad public (as in the case of media relations).

PERSONAL SELLING

Personal selling allows the organization to build customer relationships and generate sales through the use of face-to-face or other personalized presentations by the sales force (Armstrong & Kotler, 2013).

Depending on the size and structure of the organization, the customers to whom they sell, and the type of products sold, the sales function will differ. Some organizations utilize inside salespeople—individuals whose job is to meet the needs of customers who contact the organization. Examples of inside sales positions can be found in retail settings to salespeople who accept inbound telephone orders. Often, these individuals are referred to as order takers. Other organizations use outside salespeople—individuals whose job is to go out and meet clients or customers, identify their needs, and suggest a product or service solution that will meet those needs.

A wide range of examples of outside sales positions can be found in business-to-business sales, including office equipment, heavy machinery, professional services, advertising, and many others. Examples of business-to-consumer outside sales positions can include financial services and home improvement services, among others. There are exceptions; inside salespeople are compensated more heavily through an hourly or salary arrangement, while outside salespeople tend to be compensated through commissions, though some organizations use a combination of both to compensate their sales staff.

Organizations that include personal selling in their promotional mix generally understand that there are high costs associated with staffing, training, and supporting the sales force. With this in mind, the use of personal selling must be appropriate to the product or service being sold and the customer's purchasing behavior. This promotional tool is generally reserved for complex purchasing decisions.

While many organizations utilize a selling process specific to their own industry or company, the sales process typically entails seven steps, as follows (Armstrong & Kotler, 2013):

1. Prospecting and qualifying: The steps involved in identifying and qualifying potential customers for the organization.
2. Pre-approach: The activities preceding the sales call where the salesperson collects as much information as possible about the prospect prior to a meeting.
3. Approach: The initial stage in a sales interaction, when the salesperson meets the prospect for the first time. The objectives of the approach include building rapport with the prospect, gaining their attention and interest, and moving the relationship to the next phase of the selling process.
4. Presentation and/or demonstration: In this stage of the personal selling process, the salesperson transmits the information about the product and attempts to persuade the prospect to become a customer by demonstrating how the product or service being offered will solve the prospect's problem.
5. Handling objections: The actions of the salesperson to seek out, clarify, and overcome any questions or concerns raised by the prospect.
6. Closing: The culmination of a sales presentation in which a salesperson asks for the order or tries to confirm the sale.
7. Follow-up: The process of contacting the customer, after the sale, to ensure satisfaction and repeat business or handle any subsequent questions or issues. Although the sale has occurred, the follow-up step is vital to the continuation of the relationship between the organization and the customer.

An organization's use of personal selling can be an effective tool in helping the organization identify the specific needs of the buyer and carefully coordinate the resources of the company to create a customized solution to help meet those needs, thereby build a lasting relationship with the customer.

SALES PROMOTION

Sales promotion encompasses the media and nonmedia marketing strategies—applied for a predetermined, limited period of time—to consumers, retailers, or wholesalers in order to stimulate trial, increase consumer demand, or improve product availability (AMA, 2013). To clarify, sales promotion activities can be aimed at consumers or toward the marketing intermediaries. Consumer-oriented sales promotion activities are typically used to generate trial or sales, while sales promotion activities focused on retailers or wholesalers are designed to expand product distribution outlets.

This definition also makes reference to media and nonmedia strategies. This addresses the fact that a sales promotion strategy, such as a January White Sale, may utilize television advertising to communicate the sales offer to consumers. However, the short-term incentive designed to get consumers to come in and purchase bed linens is a sales promotional strategy, not an advertising strategy. To distinguish further, advertising refers to product awareness and information messaging, while sales promotion—even if communicated through a television commercial—refers to a short-term sale or incentive to purchase a product during a specific time period.

There are a number of tools marketers can use to accomplish their sales promotion objectives. Table 4.3 distinguishes consumer promotion tools from industry and business promotion tools.

DIRECT MARKETING

Direct marketing can be defined as a form of nonstore retailing that utilizes impersonal mediums, such as catalogs or direct response television ads, to communicate a product or service value proposition directly to

Table 4.3. Sales Promotion Tools

<table>
<tr><td colspan="2" align="center">Consumer Promotions</td></tr>
<tr><td>Samples</td><td>Offers of a trial amount of a product.</td></tr>
<tr><td>Coupons</td><td>Certificates that offer consumers a money savings on the purchase of a product.</td></tr>
<tr><td>Cash refunds
(rebates)</td><td>Similar to coupons, except that the price discount occurs after the purchase, rather than at the time of purchase.</td></tr>
<tr><td>Price packs
(cents-off deals)</td><td>A savings offer posted directly on the product. Can include a money-savings deal on a single product or a two-for-the-price-of-one discount.</td></tr>
<tr><td>Premiums</td><td>Additional goods that are offered either free or at a low cost as an incentive to purchase a product.</td></tr>
<tr><td>Advertising specialties</td><td>Include a wide range of promotional products imprinted with the product's name or message distributed to consumers.</td></tr>
<tr><td>Point-of-purchase
promotions</td><td>Also referred to as POP. Include displays or demonstrations at the place of sale.</td></tr>
<tr><td>Contests, sweepstakes,
and games</td><td>Promotional activities that give consumers a chance at winning something. Contests call for consumers to submit an entry, which will be judged by a panel, who will select a winner. Sweepstakes select a winner through a random drawing among all the entrants. Games present consumers with a puzzle or number every time they make a purchase, which may or may not lead to a prize.</td></tr>
<tr><td>Events/sponsorships</td><td>Creating a brand-oriented event or supporting events created by others, for the purpose of increasing awareness of the brand or product.</td></tr>
<tr><td colspan="2" align="center">Trade Promotions</td></tr>
<tr><td>Discounts</td><td>Company's discount the sale of the product to the retailer as an inducement for them to carry the product. Retailers still sell the product to the consumer at the regular price, but increase their profit on the product during the period of the discount.</td></tr>
<tr><td>Allowances</td><td>Company's offer a per-case allowance on sales made during a period in which the retailer agrees to feature the product in the store, through advertising or in-store displays, for example.</td></tr>
<tr><td>Free goods</td><td>Extra merchandise offered to retailers who agree to feature the product.</td></tr>
<tr><td>Push money</td><td>Extra money or gifts offered to dealers to encourage their sales forces to "push" the manufacturer's products.</td></tr>
<tr><td colspan="2" align="center">Business Promotions</td></tr>
<tr><td>Conventions and
trade shows</td><td>An exhibition or event in which manufacturers display their products to retailers or distributors.</td></tr>
<tr><td>Sales contests</td><td>A contest conducted for salespeople or dealers to motivate them to increase their sales performance over a particular period of time.</td></tr>
</table>

Armstrong & Kotler, 2013

consumers, enabling them to purchase the offering. Similar to sales promotion, direct marketing also seeks an immediate response from the promotional effort. The evolution of communications options has afforded direct marketers to become more and more sophisticated in their methods of contacting prospects with their offers. Early direct marketing efforts were communicated through catalogs or other mailers; this later evolved to the use of telemarketing.

Direct marketing efforts on television have also evolved significantly—moving from 30- and 60-second commercials promoting record albums or books, to program-length infomercials and cable channels, like QVC and HSN, whose programming is fully centered on direct marketing. According to the Direct Marketing Association, in 2011, American companies spend nearly $155 billion per year on direct marketing efforts—a figure that was projected to grow each year (DMA, 2011).

Some consumers have historically been suspicious of or reacted negatively to direct marketing efforts, either due to overinflated offers for products that did not live up to their promise or the complete lack of fulfillment by illegitimate businesses. Recent research has sought to investigate attitudes toward more modern direct marketing efforts, measuring attitudes toward unsolicited postal mail and email. The results indicate that respondents viewed spam as more annoying than direct mail solicitations sent through regular mail (Moromoto & Chang, 2006). Other research has focused on consumers' concerns about the privacy of the information they are sharing with direct marketers (Dolnicar & Jordaan, 2007).

Despite the attitudes toward some forms of direct marketing, consumers and companies alike realize a number of benefits from this form of promotion. For consumers, direct marketing offers convenience and privacy. Simply by examining a catalog or website, consumers have at their fingertips a multitude of products they can compare and evaluate. Though they cannot physically touch the products, they can save enormous time that would be spent driving from store to store.

Further, with today's sophisticated shipping options, consumers can receive their products quickly and conveniently at their home or office. For companies using this promotional tool, direct marketing helps streamline the distribution channel and logistics functions, resulting in a more cost-effective, efficient operation (Armstrong & Kotler, 2013). Websites, for example, afford companies greater flexibility and control over pricing offers or product descriptions. Finally, the global nature of the internet lets companies expand their reach beyond the range that could be served with a physical store location.

The variety of options through which companies can execute their direct marketing efforts are another advantage, for both the company and the consumer, offering flexibility and choice where sellers and buyers can come together to execute the value exchange. These options are reviewed in Table 4.4.

As can be seen from the review of the tools in the promotion mix, marketers have a variety of communication options they can use to implement their marketing strategy. It should be noted that not all of the tools are used for every marketing strategy. Each of the promotional tools has its strengths and weaknesses and should be used thoughtfully—in a manner that will best facilitate the value exchange. In the next section, we will review the application of these promotional tools to an educational setting.

Table 4.4.   Direct Marketing Options

Catalog marketing	Direct marketing efforts that include print, video, or digital catalogs that are mailed to select customers.
Direct mail marketing	Attempts to promote offers to customers by sending announcements or other solicitations directly to individuals via the postal service.
Direct response television marketing	An approach to the television advertising message that includes a method of response, such as an address, telephone number, or website, whereby members of the audience can respond directly to the advertiser in order to purchase a product or service offered in the advertising message. This can include short commercials, paid programming, or collaborations with direct response television networks.
Face-to-face direct marketing	Utilizing a personal selling network to directly market products to consumers. This is sometimes called network marketing.
Kiosk marketing	Using self-service ordering machines stationed in convenient, high-traffic locations to market products directly to consumers. This is sometimes called automatic vending.
Online marketing	Efforts to market products and services over the internet through websites, online ads, search engine marketing, and other web-based promotional outlets.
Telemarketing	Marketing to customers through use of the telephone, which can include both inbound and outbound selling efforts.

Armstrong & Kotler, 2013

PROMOTION FOR THE
EDUCATIONAL MARKETPLACE

Promotional activities are not new for schools, but in many cases schools have historically utilized only the public relation components of the promotional mix, with a heavy focus on communications. Given their cost effectiveness and the previous public climate that was found to be far more supportive of educational efforts, good public relations and communications were, arguably, all schools really needed to consider. As schools have become more embroiled in political conversations, community redevelopment efforts, and legislative reform efforts, promotion of your school is no longer about rallying a big crowd for Friday night's game. In order to truly maximize the promotional piece of the marketing mix, it is important to know how to effectively utilize each promotional tool for an educational context.

Advertising is expensive. It is expensive because it has the most potential to reach the largest audience. If a school has a big-picture idea, new program, or new mission that it wants everyone to know, advertising may be the way to go. However, if the cost of the advertising outweighs the potential impact on the school, a purposeful and strategic media plan should be developed. The media plan should include:

- Plan objective: What is your ultimate goal for this advertising campaign? What do you want everyone to walk away from your advertisement understanding, feeling, and doing?
- Target audience: Who is your target audience? What are their media habits? Which media forms and outlets do they utilize?
- Messaging strategy: How can schools align their plan objective with a message that the target audience will embrace? What images do you want the audience to have of the school or advertising campaign objective?
- Timeline: What is the timeline for your end goal of the advertising campaign? Does the audience have enough time to respond to your advertisement? When do you want your message to be fresh in your audience's mind? How long can you afford to run the campaign?
- Budget: How much will this advertising campaign cost? Does the school need to hire consultants, videographers, photographers, writers, or advertising agencies? What funds can you use to pay for the

campaign? Does the potential benefits of the campaign match the fiscal realities of the school?

- Assessment: Did your school meet the media plan objective? Did your school reach your target audience? Did your campaign leave the desired impression of your school on your audience? Did your messaging have the desired effect? Did you achieve your timeline? Did you stay within your budget and garner the potential benefits?

Following this basic framework for establishing an advertising campaign could be a very valuable promotional tool for schools, especially big schools with lots of stakeholders. In some cases it may be the only tool needed. In others, it may be one piece of a more dynamic mix of promotional tools. Public relation efforts allow you to tailor your message based on varying groups of stakeholders. Given that it is one of the more cost-effective forms of promotion, it is understandably one of the most utilized tools by schools. There are several facets of public relations that may be incorporated into your overall promotional activities. These could include:

- Media relations: For most schools this happens in the form of press releases, television interviews, and newspaper articles, as well as scripted public comments.
- Product publicity: Does your community see the value in what your school offers or the role your school plays in the community? When people in the community talk about your school, what do they say? When you do an internet search of your school, what pops up? How is your school portrayed in the media, excluding paid advertisements?
- Lobbying: Many schools are becoming more engaged with the political process. According to Fowler (2004),

> The current reform movement can be seen as a revolt against the aging school organization inherited from the nineteenth and early twentieth centuries and as a search for a new paradigm. . . . For the foreseeable future, the education policy scene will be turbulent with many new policy proposals, many changes, and many failed experiments. . . . When systems are in flux, individuals have a chance to exercise influence that they do not have when systems are stable. Thus, those school leaders who want to, will be able to identify those trends in their states or districts that they support and work to advance them. (p. 348)

As federal and local budgets get tighter, understanding the tenor and climate of state and federal educational policies becomes increasingly more necessary. A public school needs specific expertise in getting bonds and bond referendums on the ballot, in addition to having a voice in education reform efforts at the local, state, and federal levels. Many of the professional organizations in the field of education now have active advocacy groups.

• Investor relations: Stakeholders that make a fiscal contribution or significant impact on your school would be included in this group. Donors, alumni, families, and, in some cases, taxpayers and private corporations could all be considered investors. Schools need to engage with these groups to garner support for endowments, capital campaigns, or special events and scholarships.

• Development and maintenance of positive relations with stakeholders: Generating awareness about your school is the cornerstone of this promotional activity. It is important to raise the interest of community stakeholders in your school and the services it provides. In many ways, what has previously been known as family engagement has begun to look more like customer service.

Personal selling is the piece of the promotional mix that can be important in addressing recruitment and retention issues. Personal selling is divided into two segments, inside sales and outside sales. Gauging the experiences of your students, staff, and families with your school would be considered inside sales activities that support student retention. Outside sales would consist of your school's activities focused on the recruitment of new students, staff, and families. The importance of both recruitment and retention, as well as building a focused personal selling plan, cannot be overemphasized.

Special events, presentations, and booths at conventions; vouchers; and sample classes could all be considered educational versions of sales promotions. Some schools offer scholarships toward tuition and housing. Other schools offer free remediation, discounts on technology and clothing, or childcare services for an introductory time period. Attending extracurricular events at a reduced price or touring classes and campuses could also be considered sales promotion. Direct marketing is the most focused piece of the promotional mix.

When you have a specific message for a specific audience in a specific time frame, direct marketing is a good option. Many schools now utilize technology and social media to spread the word. School websites and social media outlets can be used to convey a message effectively and timely to share news about a weather delay, for example. For others, automatic telephone calls conveying information to stakeholders have been found effective. Many teachers utilize social media as a way to update families on class activities and provide homework support, while coaches may use it to update community members about the school's performance at out-of-state competitions.

Promotional activities require a considerable amount of resources, but, when used effectively, can yield much greater returns. With so many options in the promotional mix, aligning efforts across and within your educational institution will be crucial. The next section offers recommendations for coordinating promotional efforts across buildings and programs.

COORDINATING DISTRICT- AND BUILDING-LEVEL EFFORTS

Though most of the leadership of marketing efforts in schools, public or private, will come from either a director of communication or an administrator who works in the central office, it is important to remember the vast majority of the contacts needed for support are rooted in personal, one-on-one interactions. Political campaigns know this, and that is why they develop a broad overarching message that will be played out in television, print, and internet advertisements, but they also recruit and depend on volunteers (some who are paid) to go door-to-door to make the local contacts. Canvassing and grassroots marketing play an important role in the success of a campaign, as they help build momentum.

Remembering the importance of canvassers for political candidates is very important for schools as they develop a message. It is not so much that school district employees are expected to go door-to-door but that others may have developed a message and the teachers (playing a similar role as the canvassers) help spread the message and be the point of contact for everyone else. Typically, the person or group who develops the message cannot meet with everyone who will be impacted by the intent of the message, be it helping to recruit new students or to get a new bond measure passed.

To support a grassroots effort, there needs to be clear communication and coordination between the district and the school building. Below are some quick steps that should be employed in conveying information to building-level personnel:

1. Place a member of the building-level staff on the team developing the plan. They know the ins and outs of the day-to-day responsibilities of the building-level employees. They can talk about the time involved and discuss the typical questions that would be asked from parents and others in the community.
2. Develop a short summary of the plan. Explain the rationale behind the effort, provide some history, and explain what would happen if the plan were not put into place.
3. Develop a set of "frequently asked questions" about the proposal, with short, bulleted answers. This will make it easier for the entire team to provide consistent responses.
4. Hold an open forum where the above information is presented and any and all questions can be asked. Have the necessary people in the room who can answer the questions and address any concerns.
5. Make sure there is a person who will serve as a point of contact when there are questions.

PROMOTION IN EDUCATION

Promotion seems easier in business than in education. Many businesses know that, if they do not remain relevant and do not promote their product or service, they will not be in business anymore. Until recently, public education has had little use for promotion, with its captive audience and fairly fixed market share. But times have changed, and private, charter, and online schools are changing the landscape very dramatically.

Promotion of school efforts has also been confused with advertising. Public schools have consistently had problems with promotion. Private and charter schools have not. But public schools need to become more aware of the needs for promotion, as their districts are being affected by bond and budget issues.

The following is an example of the coordinated efforts by a district and building to prevent extensive cuts by a new school board. Though not every district faces this issue, the steps outline the concepts that should be considered when organizing a fully integrated campaign.

SCHOOL BUDGET UNDER ATTACK

Very few candidates campaign on a desire to raise taxes for schools, but it seems that many campaign to cut taxes. While public school educators cannot actively campaign for or against different candidates as a representative of the school, they can actively help the public understand the role they play in society and the benefits of a public education.

In one particular election in Pennsylvania, it seemed like all the candidates running for school board solely had as their emphasis to cut taxes and slash spending for public schools. This occurred, despite the fact that some of the schools were becoming overcrowded. All projections for the next 10 years indicated continued unsustainable growth. The middle schools and the high school had been recently updated and looked as though they could handle the increased demand, with the possible exception of crowded hallways and lunchrooms.

A few of the candidates proposed severe cuts to the school budget. Some of the candidates announced their plans over a year in advance of the election, giving time for the school leaders to plan. All indications were that the community on the whole supported the schools. However, it was an off-year election, and the school staff was concerned that only individuals *very* concerned about the local issues would show up to vote.

The superintendent and the board decided it would be good to have one member of the administrative team, the assistant superintendent for finance, and three members of the board develop a plan to educate the public about what the school does for the community. They developed a seven-point plan:

1. Leave no detail unchecked
2. Develop a simple message
3. Make it a team effort
4. Build a great plan
5. Motivate the team

6. Take the long approach to groundwork
7. Develop six very clear statements

Step 1: Leave No Detail Unchecked

Make a list of every possible question someone could ask about the public schools. Questions they came up with included:

- What are the enrollment projections for the next 10 years?
- What will be the enrollment of the new school?
- How much is spent per pupil in this district relative to other districts?
- Where does the money come from?
- How much does the state provide?
- Does the school provide special transportation to students with disabilities?
- How much money is spent on sports?
- How much money is spent on computers?
- How much does a teacher make?
- How much does an aide make?
- Where can we cut services?
- How large are class sizes?
- Is a new school necessary, or can we just use portable classrooms?
- Can we cut languages?
- Can we cut band?
- Can we cut sports?

People in the district want to see exactly what they're getting for their money. The credibility that you project with your knowledge and the people who are onboard give the community great comfort that the district spends money wisely.

Step 2: Develop a Simple Message

Most people who will be voting do not have time to read through detailed reports about overcrowding and the problems associated with too many students in a classroom. The district kept messaging simple: "Don't forget to vote to support education on November 4." This was the message given to the parents at PTO meetings, hung on the billboards outside of town, and provided for the numerous bumper stickers one saw around town. A list of FAQs were developed and posted on the district's web page to help get the information across for those who needed greater detail.

They chose this very simple message because it reminded the voters of the affirmative obligation required to support schools, that of actively going to vote on election day. They also made sure the date of the election was also included because for this election cycle there was no other state or federal office on the ballot and few seemed to be paying attention to the election.

Step 3: Make It a Team Effort

Money spent on public schools does not just affect the students and employees of the school; it affects the whole town. Therefore, they needed to highlight the benefits that healthy schools provide to the community as a whole and share the information with key community stakeholders, such as real estate agents, shopkeepers, the local chamber of commerce, builders, sports associations, local clergy, and civic groups.

Step 4: Build a Great Plan

Communication was a critical component of the plan. This included sharing information about the problems being faced by the school district as a means of justifying the need for appropriate levels of funding.

Step 5: Motivate the Team

The district and school leaders viewed their team as all the yes voters in the district—those supporting candidates for the school board who didn't want to slash the school budget. They willingly went to any and all forums they could go to and fully responded to questions from every candidate. It became clear, however, that the only candidates requesting information from the district were those who were opposed to budget cuts.

The job was to get the yes voters to the polls on the right date. There will always be voters in the district who can be referred to as CAVE (can't

accept virtually everything) voters. These voters would most likely support an increase in school funding. The job is not to convince everyone
in the district to support schools, only enough yes voters—and those who
could potentially be convinced to become yes voters.

Step 6: Take the Long Approach to Groundwork

The district realized they may have priorities, but those priorities may not
be the same as what the electorate is willing to fund. To identify public
priorities, polling was conducted. Polling can be very useful to identify
the depth of public support for a particular issue. For example, the football
stadium may be crumbling, and the support for a new stadium may be
very vocal but not very deep. This would be an indication of something
the electorate would be unlikely to support.

Step 7: Develop Six Very Clear Statements

The team developed a series of simple statements about the school. The
ability to inject positive comments about an institution that has taken a
beating in public opinion is very important. These were short, memorable
sentences focused on a single topic that could be easily incorporated into
a conversation with a constituent. Here are some examples of statements:

- We provide a comprehensive reading, math, music, and arts program
  for all our students.
- Over 85 percent of our students graduate from school.
- Over 65 percent of our students go on to higher education.
- Sixty-five percent of our teachers hold master's degrees or higher.
- Many of our teachers have become experts in their field and have taught
  over 10 years.
- We have a new program to attract young, talented teachers to our schools.
- We have one of the best sets of test scores of any schools in our area.
- We have over 100 applicants for each teaching job. We take only the best.
- Our school debate team is one of the best in the state.
- Our (pick a sport) sports team is one of the best in the state.
- Our district made Annual Yearly Progress last year. We are very proud
  of that.

- We offer more electives at our high school than most schools.
- Our students get into the colleges they want to go to.
- We have a security plan that is very good, and the teachers are continually trained for emergencies.

The League of Women Voters sponsored a debate for all the candidates. It became very clear the only candidates aware of what was going on in the schools were the candidates who had talked with school officials about the need for certain subjects and expenditures. The audience was filled with teachers and school administrators. The candidates who wanted to slash the school budget could not come up with specifics to cut, other than "fat" or "waste." The other candidates, however, spoke eloquently about the need for, and continued support of, current and continued expenditures for public education.

As a result of the coordinated public education campaign, those candidates who supported the current school budget were elected handily. School leaders took the election results as a sign of public affirmation. The district realized the need for ongoing awareness within the community about what they do and committed to maintaining open communication, rather than waiting for the next challenge.

CONCLUSION

Promotion is difficult for some schools to understand. However, it is a vital part of the process for schools to send the appropriate messages to an audience. This is a very important shift in thinking for today's school leaders in order to realize operational success.

CASE STUDY:
The Paramount Health Data Project

One of the cornerstones of the charter school movement is the opportunity for small, autonomous schools to leverage their autonomy to cultivate innovative best practices. In many ways, the promise of autonomy leading to innovation has been a difficult promise to keep. The reality of navigating the day-to-day hustle and bustle of running a freestanding school can be overwhelming even for the most savvy of educators. One school on the eastside of Indianapolis has managed to not only grow one of the highest-preforming schools in the state but also incubate an innovative practice that has the potential to change the landscape of education and health care.

Paramount Schools of Excellence (PSOE) with a 90 percent free and reduced lunch percentage and 18 percent special education population, earned an A from the Indiana Department of Education and was named an Indiana Four Star School for excellence and a National Blue Ribbon School by the US Department of Education in 2018. PSOE also boasts the highest achievement scores for students with individualized education programs (IEPs) in the state. They also served as a visit site for the National School Based Health Alliance Annual conference as an example of best practices and earned more than $1 million in external award dollars to support a specific project taking place across the school.

How is a small K–8 charter school earning notoriety from national health organizations? How are they beating every other school in the state on academic achievement tests for students with IEPs? They are focused on differentiation in a whole new way. PSOE has developed a partnership with a local health care agency and received funding to support the infusion of health data into their MTSS process. A typical MTSS process follows a basic process that includes the elements in Figure 4.1.

As part of the Paramount Health Data Project (PHDP), student health data is also part of the data stream, providing additional data to aid in the implementation of MTSS interventions. This data is analyzed and summarized to ensure that each student is given the level of academic support they need. In most schools implementing MTSS, the crucial work of synthesizing data is performed by the MTSS coordinator. This position is held by a school staff member who has expertise in data-driven instruction and student supports. The integration of student health data into this

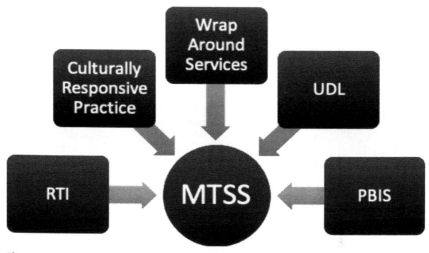

Figure 4.1. MTSS process

process necessitates additional training and structures to ensure that all relevant FERPA and HIPPA regulations are met. Once these additional forms have been completed during enrollment processes, PSOE is able to correlate the student's health data with their academic achievement data.

The PHDP is based on the premise that there is an interaction between health, poverty, and education that impacts overall health and wellness. Since 2013 PSOE Brookside has been implementing the University of Tennessee's Consortium for Health Education, Economic Empowerment, and Research (CHEER) data collection protocols for all visits to their nurse's office. This has allowed PSOE Brookside to build a longitudinal data set with more than 300,000 data points specifically related to the health and educational outcomes of students visiting the nurse's office. An initial analysis of this large data set revealed a statistically significant relationship between the number of times a student visits the school nurse and a decrease in academic achievement over time, as measured by Acuity, a standardized academic assessment. Students who were frequent visitors to the school nurse (eight or more times) showed significantly lower test scores than occasional visitors (seven or fewer times). These differences in test scores were seen in the results of the beginning of year testing (BOY), continued through the middle of year testing (MOY), and were present at the end of year (EOY) testing. The significantly higher test scores were seen in both mathematics and language arts, although the differences between frequent visitors and occasional visitors were much greater in language arts than in mathematics. Further analysis revealed that specific diagnoses that correlated to diseases of poverty, specifically neurological diagnoses such as tension headaches, gastrointestinal diagnoses such as gastric reflux, and dermatological diagnoses such as rashes, accounted for an up to a 10 percent decrease in testing scores (Figure 4.2).

Based on these initial findings, PSOE has begun the process of integrating student health data into the MTSS process on a regular basis. As noted above, the MTSS coordinator works with the teaching staff to gather and interpret student data to determine whether a Tier 2 intervention is needed and what intervention should be implemented. The MTSS process is most effective when there is enough data to determine the need for an intervention as early as possible in the academic year. Because the standardized academic assessment is given in the middle of the year, the use of student health data triggers interventions sooner than would happen when relying on the academic assessment calendar.

These additional pieces of data are enabling PSOE to ensure that their academic practices are as evidence based and informed as possible. PSOE leadership has navigated two completely different social systems, public schools and private health care, in a way that has not been done before. By truly leveraging their autonomy as a charter school, they've been able to innovate their federally required MTSS processes for the betterment of children.

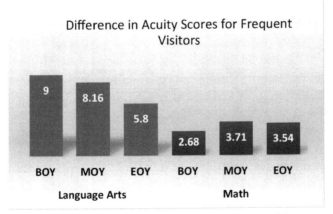

Figure 4.2.   Difference in Acuity Scores for Frequent Visitors

As schools like PSOE create new promising best practices, the need to be able to share these practices across multiple audiences becomes more prevalent. PSOE has worked with researchers and marketers to ensure that the PHDP can be shared more broadly. Important special projects, like this, should have a place in your marketing mix efforts.

REFERENCES

American Marketing Association (AMA). (2013). Dictionary. Retrieved from http://www.marketingpower.com/_layouts/Dictionary.aspx?dLetter=A.

Armstrong, G., & Kotler, P. (2013). *Marketing: An introduction* (11th ed.). Boston, MA: Pearson.

Baack, D. (1997). *Organizational behavior.* Houston, TX: Dame Publications.

Calder, B. (2008). *Kellogg on advertising and media.* Hoboken, NJ: John Wiley & Sons.

Clow, K., & Baack, D. (2001). *Integrated advertising, promotion, and marketing communications.* Upper Saddle River, NJ: Prentice Hall.

Direct Marketing Association. (2011). *DMA 2011 statistical fact book* (33rd ed.). New York: Direct Marketing Association.

Dolnicar, S., & Jordaan, Y. (2007). A market-oriented approach to responsibly managing information privacy concerns in direct marketing. *Journal of Advertising, 35*(2), 123–149.

Fowler, F. C. (2004). *Policy studies for educational leaders: An introduction.* Upper Saddle River, NJ: Pearson.

Kotler, P., & Keller, K. (2012). *Marketing management* (14th ed.). Boston, MA: Prentice Hall.

Moromoto, M., & Chang, S. (2006). Consumers' attitudes toward unsolicited commercial e-mail and postal direct mail marketing methods: Intrusiveness, perceived loss of control, and irritation. *Journal of Interactive Advertising, 7*(1), 8–20.

Public Relations Society of America (PRSA). (n.d.). About public relations. Retrieved from http://www.prsa.org/AboutPRSA/PublicRelationsDefined/.

Chapter Five

Social Media Marketing

We don't have a choice on whether we do social media, the question is how well we do it.

—Erik Qualman, equalman.com

Social media has become infused into the culture. On both personal and professional levels, social media has grown in both the number of outlets and users. According to Pew Research Center, social media usage rates among US adults are as high as 94 percent for YouTube and 80 percent for Facebook (Smith & Anderson, 2018). While Facebook remains dominant among all adults, usage rates vary by platform depending on age, with adults aged 18 to 24 more likely to use Snapchat and Instagram (CITE). Other demographic variables can impact usage as well. For example, women are more likely to visit Pinterest, LinkedIn is more likely to be used by those with college degrees, and WhatsApp is more popular with Hispanic Americans.

Worldwide, the number of active monthly users of social media has grown from nearly 1 billion in 2010, to 2.46 billion in 2017. That number is expected to top 3 billion by 2021. Geographically, social media penetration is greatest in North America, with approximately 70 percent of the population having one or more social media accounts. In the United States, 81 percent of the population maintains a profile on a social networking platform (Clement, 2019).

The growth in both platforms and users presents challenges and opportunities for organizations looking to incorporate social media marketing into their overall promotional strategy. This chapter will discuss the key components educational leaders should consider when planning and implementing social media marketing campaigns.

MANAGERIAL CONSIDERATIONS
OF SOCIAL MEDIA BEHAVIOR

Digital marketing strategist David Chaffey introduced a definition of social media marketing: "Monitoring and facilitating customers' interaction, participation and sharing through digital media to encourage positive engagement with a company and its brands leading to commercial value. Interactions may occur on a company site, social networks and other third party websites" (Chaffey, 2002, p. 7).

The evolution and growth of the internet has significantly changed the manner in which marketing communication flows. Print and broadcast mediums emphasize one-way communication that streams from the sender to the receiver. Today's Web 2.0 digital communication enables information to move not only back and forth between senders and receivers, but across to other people as well. Referred to as the horizontal revolution, social media has cultivated a marketplace where consumers create content, convey information, and collaborate with others. By its very nature, social media encourages a culture of participation and engagement (Tuten & Solomon, 2013).

As a marketing tool, social media offers several benefits, including customer engagement, relationship building, information dissemination, and enhanced reach and targeting (Venciute, 2018). Social media provides opportunities for interactions between the organization and the customer, as well as for customer-to-customer communication. Access to information, combined with engagement, deepens an individual's connection to a brand or company and can lead to increased loyalty. From a management perspective, social media keeps the organization more closely connected to the dynamic marketplace, enabling the firm to have real-time access to information and feedback.

The notion of engaging with customers in an open, online forum is often challenging for many organizations, as it requires them to give up complete control of the messaging and engage in dialogic communication. While many marketers may believe the inversion of top-down marketing communication leads to an increase in vulnerability for the organization, some researchers argue that this actually leads to a more engaging and potentially more satisfying customer experience (Prahalad & Ramaswamy, 2004).

THE DIGITAL MARKETING LANDSCAPE

Many have suggested a fifth *P* be added the 4*P*s of the marketing mix, such as *people, processes*, and *philosophy*. Practically speaking, the evolution of social media introduces *participation* as a key component of the marketing mix. Participation happens when users engage with content on a social media platform. Nearly 209 million people in the United States use one or more forms of social media every month. In 2018, advertising revenue on social media platforms exceeded $26.6 million (Social Media Advertising).

There are two ways to reach an audience on social media: organic and paid. Organic social media involves the use of a social media platform's tools to build and interact with a community. This includes sharing content and responding to the content or posts of others in the community. Organic social media helps an organization build and interact with an audience on an ongoing basis. Examples include maintaining Facebook and Twitter pages or a YouTube channel.

Paid social media includes the use of sponsored messages or boosted posts to reach a defined audience. Typically, the cost of the advertising is tied to the number of people who respond to the ad, referred to as cost per click. Paid social programs offer a targeted and extremely affordable channel for budget-conscious organizations to advertise. Paid advertising campaigns can be scheduled with the advertising tools available on social platforms, such as Facebook Ads Manager.

Paid social media advertising can play just one part in an organization's digital marketing strategy. In addition to social media advertising options, there are a wide variety of digital advertising options available to marketers. Table 5.1 describes the various digital advertising categories.

Educational leaders are often intimidated by the language used in social media management. Table 5.2 displays a list of some of the most commonly used social media marketing terms.

Table 5.1. Digital Advertising Categories

Digital Option	Description
Search engine advertising	Sponsored results that show up when a user performs a keyword search on a search engine, such as Google or Bing.
Display advertising	Advertising that appears on websites that permit ads, including banner, overlay, and rich media ads.
Mobile advertising	Advertising that appears on mobile devices such as smartphones or tablets. Examples include banner or embedded ads in downloaded apps or mobile games.
Video advertising	Online ads that feature video that occurs before, during, or after a video stream on the internet.
Cross-channel advertising	The dissemination of paid messages to prospects across a variety of digital marketing channels.

Table 5.2. Social Media Marketing Terminology

Term	Definition
Algorithm	A system that suggests pages to search engines in response to a search query.
Analytics	Data from social media websites.
Blog	A regularly updated website or web page that is written in an informal or conversational style.
Chatbot	Chatbots are a type of bot that lives in messaging apps (like Facebook Messenger) and use artificial intelligence to perform tasks via simulated conversation. They can be used for customer service, data collection, and more.
Click through rate (CTR)	A common social media metric calculated by looking at the number of people who click a link in a piece of content divided by the number of people who saw the content.
Content management system (CMS)	A software application or program that is used to create, modify, and manage digital content.
Dark social	Any social media content that is shared outside of what can be measured by analytics, for example sharing a blog post link via email or text.
Engagement rate	The percentage of people who saw and actively interacted with social media content, such as clicked a link, expanded an image, commented, liked, shared, retweeted, etc.
Employee advocate	An employee who is willing to promote and defend a company online and off. Employees can influence the purchasing decisions of friends, family, and other social contacts.
Employee amplification	The resharing of a company's social content by its employees. Amplification programs are used to leverage employee advocates at scale to greatly increase the social reach of a brand.
Feed	A news feed of updates and content posted by other social media users, including individuals and businesses.
Follow	Subscribing to the updates of fellow users. Typically applies to Twitter and Instagram.

Term	Definition
Follower	Subscribing to the updates of fellow users. Typically applies to Twitter and Instagram.
Following	Users whose feeds you subscribe to. Typically applies to Twitter and Instagram.
Hashtag	A word or phrase preceded by the # sign. They serve as a simple way to market a topic of social media messages and make them discoverable to people with shared interests.
Lurker	A user of a social media site or message board who consumes information readily but does not regularly or actively contribute via posts, conversations, or other means.
Platform	A system that manages content. For instance, WordPress is a platform that manages a community of blogs, while LinkedIn supports professional networking and job searches.
Retargeting	An online advertising technique that involves target web visitors who expressed an interest in your product or service. It involves placing a tracking tag on the website, which enables the organization to target visitors to the website as they visit other websites, including Facebook, news sites, or other online media.
Search engine optimization (SEO)	The process of organizing your website to give it the best chance of appearing near the top of search engine rankings.
Search engine marketing (SEM)	A form of internet marketing that involves the promotion of websites by increasing their visibility in search engine result pages primarily through paid advertising.
Social media optimization (SMO)	The use of a number of outlets and communities to generate publicity to increase the awareness of a product, service, brand, or event.
Thread	An individual conversational trail within a social media platform, forum, or bulletin board, typically beginning with an original post and continuing with comments and conversation attached to that original post.
Traffic	The number of visitors who visit a website.
Trending	A word, phrase, or topic that is popular on Twitter at a given moment.
Trending	The most popular topics and hashtags on a social media site. These often become clickable links that users can select to view or join the larger conversation.
Troll	A user who is known for purposely posting inflammatory content with the intent of creating controversy on a social media platform.
User-generated content (UGC)	Content that is created by consumers/customers.
Uniform resource locator (URL)	The location of a page or other resource on the World Wide Web.
Viral	Anything shared across social networks that gets passed along rapidly. YouTube videos are a great example.
Vlog	A blog in which the postings are primarily in video form.

DEVELOPING A SOCIAL MEDIA
MARKETING STRATEGY

Due to the large number of people who engage with social media plat-forms on a daily basis, sophisticated marketers have moved many of their promotional efforts to the digital space. According to the Nielsen Com-pany, in 2018, Americans spent an average of 11 hours per day engaging with some form of media content, including television, radio, print, or online material (Nielsen, 2018). Users spend an average of two hours, fifteen minutes of their overall media time on social media (Cohen, 2018).

Recognizing that social media marketing is a component of the orga-nization's overall marketing plan, a social media marketing strategy calls for management to understand the customer, secure the resources avail-able to implement a campaign, and identify a clear goal (Paswan, 2018). The organization's marketing plan should already have the description of the target audience(s) in mind. Many organizations already have exist-ing social media pages. The analytics resources available on the social platform can identify basic demographic data of the community. To the extent that the social media is reaching the desired audience, an objective would be to continue to grow the audience through organic strategies. Conversely, if the organization is seeking to reach more of its desired audience, a paid social marketing campaign may be in order.

If a paid social campaign is in order, to promote a specific event, for example, an open house, the overall marketing plan should outline the budget that can be allocated for digital advertising. In terms of allocating resources for paid social media advertising, of the overall marketing bud-get, organizations typically allocate 35 to 45 percent to digital marketing activities. Of that digital allocation, anywhere from 15 to 25 percent is usually spent on social media marketing efforts (Kendig, 2018). However, the budgetary shift toward digital marketing efforts continues to grow. A recent survey of chief marketing officers in the US indicates that digital ad spending will grow more than 12 percent in 2019 (Steimer, 2019).

The overall marketing plan will identify goals to be achieved for the organization. The social media marketing strategy will serve as a promo-tional channel to achieve the overall goal(s). The overall marketing plan for a school may identify enrollment rates as a goal. Toward that goal, an open house may serve as a support tactic. The promotion of an open house may include radio and yard signs, as well as organic and paid social media. Sample goals for the social media could include increased visits to the social media page or increased clicks from social media to the open house page on the school's website.

Once the goals are established, the strategy needs to outline topics and specific content that will be published to support the campaign. Digital marketing content can be broken out into three categories: informational, engagement, and promotional. Informational content includes postings, infographics, videos, podcasts, and blogs. Engagement content is interactive. Examples include quizzes, posing questions, or asking for postings (user-generated content).

Promotional content can be used to drive conversions, such as getting prospective parents to click through to the website to register to attend an informational breakfast. However, promotional content can also be used to increase awareness of events across a variety of platforms. For example, asking your followers to tag and share photos to promote spirit of a team going through playoffs can be a way of both engaging followers and promoting a particular theme, such as *#StateChampsBound*! Promotional content also includes paid or sponsored content displayed on social platforms.

Scheduling the distribution of content is also important. Many organizations new to social media share all content equally across all platforms. The creation of an editorial calendar will help manage the distribution of content to the relevant audience in a timely fashion. The social media editorial calendar should serve as a support vehicle for the organization's overall marketing timeline. Typically organizations will plan their social media calendar a quarter at a time, allowing enough flexibility for new developments or opportunities. Table 5.3 displays a sample format for a social media content calendar.

Table 5.3. Sample Social Media Content Calendar

Log				Facebook *(add section for each social platform used)*		
Date	Day	Time	Notes	Message	Link	Visual
8/13/18	Mon	9:00 am	Enter notes	Enter message	URL link	Describe photo, video, or infographic

BUILDING AN AUDIENCE

Today's internet-savvy customers are generally accustomed to performing online searches before they engage with a brand or make a purchase. Successful brands seek to be recognized on internet search engine results as well as on social media. A key component of an organization's social media marketing strategy is audience development. As Figure 5.1 suggests, social media audience members can be classified into three groupings.

Committed audience members are passionate about the organization. For schools, they should include faculty and staff, board members, foundation staff and board, students, families, and alumni. These should be the early adopters of the organization's social media community and represent the most active participants, those who like, comment, and share content. Connected audience members know about the organization and are strong advocates. This could include a mix of families, alumni, and possibly vendors or other organizations with whom the organization regu-

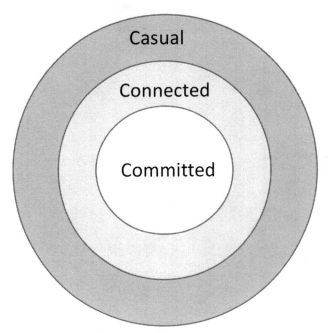

Figure 5.1.   Social Media Audience Segments

larly interacts. Individuals in this group should take very little convincing to follow the organization on social media.

Engagement with members of this category will depend on the level of interest in the topic of content posted on the social media site. For example, alumni may not be interested in postings about the football team, but they may be interested in sharing information about an upcoming reunion. Casual members of the social media audience could include families, alumni, former staff members, and people who live in the community, especially prospective school families. Participation by members of this group will most likely be limited to lurking activity. Although they are not actively engaged, they are exposed to the information being posted to the social media page.

Posting engaging content is the best way to increase an organization's reach on social media. Members of the community are more apt to like, comment on, and share content they find interesting and useful. Once those followers engage with the organization's content, the power of social networking takes over, and the original post is then exposed to those individuals who are connected to the organization's community. For organizations new to social media marketing, asking employees or board members to share content is an effective strategy. Having quality members of the social media community, those who actively participate, has a multiplier effect on organization's social media impact. Other methods for growing a social media following include:

- Making sure the profiles of the organization's social media accounts are complete. That way, if a person searches a relevant keyword on a social platform, the organization will appear in the results.
- Promoting the social media platform icons (Twitter, Facebook, LinkedIn, YouTube, etc.) by making sure they are visible on the organization's website, employee email signatures, and business cards.
- Embedding a direct link to the organization's social media page in other posted content, such as blogs.
- Promoting the social media community off-line at in-person events. People who engage with the school community in person will be more likely to follow the organization on social media.
- Using hashtags to increase the visibility of posts on Instagram and Twitter. Hashtags make the content more easily searched on the platform.

- Engaging with followers by posting replies, tagging, and sharing.
- Posting more visual content. People engage more regularly with photos and videos.

Some organizations will often create multiple profiles on the same social media platform. This strategy should be approached with caution. Large organizations with a portfolio of brands will be more successful with this strategy, as it is more common for a consumer to follow a brand, as opposed to the corporation. In the case of schools, creating too many communities within a single platform serves to splinter the audience, which undermines the organization's ability to reach a large audience. The possible exception to this might be to establish a separate social media profile for athletics, as is a common practice for some schools to post game outcomes and other content about individual athletes or teams.

CONTENT IS KING

The type of content posted to the organization's social media accounts will depend on the objective the organization is trying to achieve. Most content falls within three broad categories: early stage, midstage, and late stage (Marketo, n.d.). Early-stage messages can include lighthearted entertaining, as well as educational content. Midstage messages are more goal focused and could include contests, invitations, and free material, such as newsletters or white papers. A private school, for example, may offer a free e-book discussing the value and affordability of private school education. This approach helps deepen the relationship with prospective parents who become more engaged with the school and willingly provide their personal information, something that is challenging for marketing practitioners in this day of digital privacy and permissions-based marketing.

Permission marketing refers to a promotional practice in which the prospect agrees in advance to receive marketing information.

Research has suggested that the customer response to social media messaging is a function of the individual's personal motivation, behavior, and the messaging content (Hoffman, Novak, & Kang, 2016). However, it is not clear which types of content generate the greatest impact on engagement or brand connectedness.

A variety of content can help distinguish the organization's brand personality. White papers and blogs can communicate thought leadership. Infographics can share data-driven value messages. Photos and videos can be both entertaining and informative. Tip sheets or checklists can drive customer behavior. Some schools will also involve their students in the creation of content as a means of conveying the school's culture or brand. In fact, research involving student-generated content at the university level suggests that such content has positive implications for recruiting and enrollment purposes, as prospective students and families will often investigate the school's social media to gain a sense of the student life experience (Brook, 2016).

While visual content can help with engagement, one study of Facebook posts by the world's top 100 brands suggests that the optimal results employ a mix of visual content and intriguing text strategies to encourage a conversation (Brubaker & Wilson, 2018). For schools, which are human-centered organizations, the combination of visuals with storytelling is often a powerful strategy to drive engagement.

> Brand storytelling utilizes authentic stories by the organization to drive customer growth and loyalty.

Video storytelling, as compared to a more sales-focused execution, has been shown to result in more favorable attitudes toward a brand, as well as generate more favorable responses and shares on social media (Coker, Flight, & Baima, 2017). Further, story-formatted content can be up to 20 times more memorable (Latham, 2018).

There are a number of best practices that should be taken into consideration when using video storytelling on social media. First, the story needs to be simple and clear and harness the emotion of the audience. The audio needs to be of high quality and visuals need to be explanatory. In addition, since many people do not use the sound on their smart devices, most stories include subtitles for people to read. Finally, the content needs to include a call to action for the audience to either post a comment or visit a website to obtain more information (Latham, 2018).

MANAGING THE SOCIAL MEDIA EFFORT

Beyond planning a social media calendar and creating content, there are a number of components that factor into an organization's social media marketing plan. Because social media involves interactive communication, there must be a dedicated staff member who will not only manage the social media function and schedule posts but also monitor the platforms for content that needs to be responded to, or otherwise shared, as well as manage any paid social media marketing activity.

From an organizational perspective, many organizations create a social media governance board, which can include key staff, stakeholders, and those individuals who would be willing to serve as social media advocates. In the case of schools, this could include a mix of teachers, as well as parents. Most organizations today, especially school districts, have social media policies that cover employees and provide regular training to key individuals who serve as social media communicators. For example, many school districts prohibit faculty and staff from friending or following students enrolled in the district. The Social Media Governance website provides a free database of social media policies for a variety of industries. It is accessible at www.socialmedia governance.com/policies.

Other policy considerations for schools include the degree to which social media interferes with the Family Educational Rights and Privacy Act (FERPA). School personnel have been advised, "not to use their personal phones, email accounts, Twitter or other social media accounts, and other personal technology to communicated with other staff, students, parents, or teachers about students" (Crowley, 2013, paras. 13, 14).

School leaders must also consider the investment the organization will commit to a social media marketing strategy. Within the context of the organization's overall marketing effort, the addition of a social media marketing strategy will have implications for staffing due to the fact that social media requires ongoing attention. With that in mind, schools should determine how many platforms will be utilized and project the level of time required to manage the social media marketing effort.

Any paid social media marketing must also be incorporated into the overall marketing plan and budget. For nonprofit organizations, Google offers $10,000 of in-kind Google advertising per month through its

Ad Grants program (https://www.google.com/intl/ALL/grants/). Eligible nonprofit organizations can apply to take advantage of the search engine advertising as a way to reach an audience. If a public school or school corporation is deemed ineligible, they may be able to partner with their nonprofit educational foundation to take advantage of this opportunity.

Social media use by schools has become more widely adopted as a communications channel, as the perceived benefits outweigh the drawbacks. Because social media enables schools to communicate in real time, school leaders are able to disseminate information to stakeholders in a more timely and efficient manner. Research by Lewis (2017) noted that the address and phone contact information for families can change with no notice to the school, but that social media pages remain constant. In addition, "Facebook can be in any language, so if a parent has difficulty reading communication shared, it is likely their Facebook page is in their native language (Lewis, 2017, p. 36). The timeliness and ability to engage in two-way dialogue with stakeholder groups ultimately helps solidify the relationship between schools and the communities they serve.

EVALUATION

When people interact with social media platforms, they leave a social footprint. Recognizing this, teachers and parents caution students about the comments and photos they post to social media. The same holds true for organizations, which should also be mindful of the imprint they are leaving on the internet (Rotsztein, 2013). Organizations should begin to manage their digital footprint by performing an audit of the sites where they engage with the public to see what results have been indexed by a search engine such as Google.

On a regular basis, such as quarterly and annually, the results of social media marketing activity should be measured. There are a number of metrics that organizations should monitor on a regular basis. Each platform has its insights or an analytics function that will enable the organization to monitor performance results.

- Social network followers: For each social platform being maintained, the number of followers or fans should be regularly calculated.

- Social network post reach: The analytics function will also display the number of people reached by the organization's posts, either paid or organic.
- Engagement: The level of engagement per post can be measured in impressions, as well as by clicks, reactions, comments, and shares.

The results of paid social media marketing efforts can be measured through the social platform's advertising management function. Key performance metrics to monitor include total reach, as well as the level of engagement (either blogs or views for videos), and the total spent. Paid social media can be an extremely efficient way of reaching an audience, with the average cost per contact (either click or view) generally measured in pennies for Facebook. The cost per action for Google AdWords advertising can vary, though the advertiser can set the budget parameters they are willing to pay, both in total spend and per action.

In addition to tracking the metrics from social network platforms, schools should also monitor the metrics of their website. Google Analytics provides a number of valuable insights into how people find and use the website. There are numerous features of Google Analytics. There are some basic metrics school leaders should examine on a regular basis.

- Sessions: The total number of visits to the website for a particular time period.
- Users: The number of unduplicated visitors to the website for a particular time period. This can be broken down to new and returning visitors.
- Pageviews: The total number of pages seen by visitors to the website for a particular time period.
- Pages/session: The average number of pages a user visits per session.
- Average session duration: The average time visitors spend viewing the website.
- Bounce rate: The percentage of users who visit only one page on the website before exiting.
- Behavioral page views: The top pages (by title or URL) users visit on the website.
- Keywords: The search terms users typed in their browser to find the website. This can inform a search engine optimization and/or a paid search advertising strategy.

- Site search terms: The terms visitors type into a search box within the website to find content.
- Device usage: There are a number of metrics that break out website visits by device (desktop, tablet, mobile), including most active days of the week, number of users, and pages per session.
- Location: The geographic location of the visitors to the website (country, state, city).
- Traffic sources: The online source that directed visitors to the website, such as a social media platform.
- Conversion rates: A measure of actions visitors take on the website, such as registering to attend an event or signing up to receive information.

The insights gained from website and social media platform analytics can inform future marketing planning and social media content calendars.

CASE STUDY:
Agora

Agora Cyber Charter School is an online K–12 public charter school that serves about 6,000 students across the entire Commonwealth of Pennsylvania. As a public school, the authorizing agency for Agora is the Pennsylvania Department of Education (PDE). Agora was first launched in 2004, run and operated by a management company. In 2014 the board of trustees voted to be a self-managed school. As a school of choice, and a virtual school in particular, there are a myriad of reasons why families choose to enroll their children at Agora: real or perceived shortcomings of a previous school, more flexibility to participate in opportunities such as sports or music, have a fresh start due to dealing with bullying or other social challenges, and for services they believe the school is better designed to meet, especially with students in need of special education services.

A new senior leadership team took shape in the latter half of 2016, at which time focus was given to developing a wider and more targeted social media presence. This plan was designed to help Agora better communicate its story and the story of the students and families that choose to attend the school. Since 2016 there have been so many positive changes that have taken place, as seen in improvements in state testing scores, student growth metrics, and improvements in school climate. To this end, the social media plan was not designed solely to increase enrollment and marketing efforts, but it had a wider focus of communicating its brand. Internally, leadership used themes such as "moving forward" and "No apologies. No excuses. We are making a difference" to communicate the positive changes that were occurring.

Agora partnered with an outside public relations and marketing firm to assist it in organizing its social media tone of voice and in creating smart content that aligns with its values; from this, the evergreen hashtag #AgoraProud was launched. By using this hashtag, there has been a sizable spike in engagement across all the social media channels, in particular with Instagram, which saw likes on posts double.

Agora also has begun to develop a new brand theme: "Chart a new course." This retells the story of the school's continuous, significant, and systemic course of change to improve its services in preparing all learners to achieve their highest potential, which is the core of the school's vision statement. While at the same time, "chart a new course" also reiterates a central theme in its marketing, which is Agora is a place where students can start fresh in their pursuit to chart a new course in engaging in their schooling, achieving their personal learning goals, and cultivating success as lifelong learners.

A significant part of the branding effort utilized digital media, through use of the school's website, Facebook, Twitter, and Instagram accounts. The tone of voice that Agora uses reinforces #AgoraProud by keeping the posts positive, friendly, and approachable. The desire is for these postings to be informative but also to craft a message that easily identifies the core values of Agora. The majority of posts seek to communicate the various activities occurring in the school and to inform the community on teacher and student successes.

Analysis of metrics of what posts receive the highest interactions and views reveal that this is what people are looking for, to see the celebrations and information of what is happening in the school. Some of the posts with the highest interaction relate to the regional proms Agora hosts each year, the graduation ceremony held at an arena in the central part of the state, and a weekly informative feature called #WhyAgoraWednesday. During graduation 2018, Agora's social media saw about 1,500 impressions from the posts, which is beneficial in broadening the scope of its audience. Overall, since instituting this social media campaign, Agora has seen a 37 percent increase in engagement.

In all of these, great care is given to avoid the posts sounding promotional, but rather to invite people into the conversation of why the school is #AgoraProud. Agora believes having a platform for the school and its families to share stories of success is paramount. Since many students come to Agora who have struggled in another setting, albeit for academic, social, emotional, or other reasons, it resonates with people when they can empathize and relate to the way the school provides an opportunity for them to chart a new course and overcome those barriers.

REFERENCES

Abram, C. (2008, August 26). Our first 100 million. Retrieved from https://www.facebook.com/notes/facebook/our-first-100-million/28111272130/.

Brook, Z. (2016). Student-generated posts power St. Lawrence University's social media. Retrieved from https://www.ama.org/publications/eNewsletters/Pages/how-one-college-uses-students-to-power-social-marketing.aspx.

Brubaker, P., & Wilson, C. (2018). Let's give them something to talk about: Global brands' use of visual content to drive engagement and build relationships. *Public Relations Review, 44*(3), 342–352.

Chaffey, D. (2002). *E-business and e-commerce management* (6th ed.). Harlow: Pearson Education.

Clement, J. (2019). Social media statistics & facts. Retrieved from https://www.statista.com/topics/1164/social-networks/.

Cohen, H. (2018). 2018 Media use has changed: What you need to do. Retrieved from https://heidicohen.com/2018-social-media-use-research/.

Coker, K., Flight, R., & Baima, D. (2017). Skip it or view it: The role of video storytelling in social media marketing. *Marketing Management Journal, 27*(2), 75–87.

Crowley, B. (2013, February 20). Are emails, texts, tweets, and other digital communications student records under FERPA and state law? Retrieved from http://edlawinsights.com/2013/02/20/are-emails-textstweetsandotherdigital-communicationsstudentrecords-under-ferpa-and-state-law/.

Hendricks, D. (2013). Complete history of social media: Then and now. Retrieved from https://smallbiztrends.com/2013/05/the-complete-history-of-social-media-infographic.html.

Hoffman, D., Novak, T., & Kang, H. (2016). Let's get closer: Feelings of connectedness from using social media with implications for brand outcomes. Retrieved from https://ssrn.com/abstract=2728281.

Kendig, P. (2018). How to set a realistic social media advertising budget. Retrieved from https://www.webstrategiesinc.com/blog/how-to-set-a-realistic-social-advertising-budget.

Latham, M. (2018). Top 10 best practices for multimedia storytelling. Retrieved from https://www.cision.com/us/2018/10/10-best-practices-multimedia-storytelling/.

Lewis, B. (2017). Experiences of leaders in one Texas school district integrating social media as a communication medium: Bounded phenomenological case study (Doctoral dissertation, Lamar University). ProQuest.

Marketo. (n.d.). The definitive guide to social media marketing. Retrieved from https://www.marketo.com/definitive-guides/the-definitive-guide-to-social-media-marketing/.

Nielsen. (2018). Time flies: US adults now spending nearly half a day interacting with media. https://www.nielsen.com/us/en/insights/article/2018/time-flies-us-adults-now-spend-nearly-half-a-day-interacting-with-media/.

Paswan, A. (2018). Social media marketing strategies. *Journal of Contemporary Research in Management,* January.

Prahalad, C. K., & Ramaswamy, V. (2004). Co-creating unique value with customers. *Strategy & Leadership, 32*(3), 4–9.

Rotsztein, B. (2013). Managing your social footprint. Retrieved from https://www.socialmediatoday.com/content/managing-your-social-media-footprint.

Smith, A., & Anderson, M. (2018). Social media use in 2018. Retrieved from http://www.pewinternet.org/2018/03/01/social-media-use-in-2018/.

Steimer, S. (2019). Dream less, do more: 2019 Marketing predictions. Retrieved from https://www.ama.org/marketing-news/dream-less-do-more-2019-marketing-predictions/.

Tuten, T., & Solomon, M. (2013). *Social media marketing.* Upper Saddle River, NJ: Pearson Education.

VanDijck, J. (2013). *The culture of connectivity: A critical history of social media.* New York, NY: Oxford University Press.

Venciute, D. (2018). Social media marketing: From tool to capability. *Management of Organizations: Systematic Research, 79,* 131–145.

Zolkepli, I., & Kamarulzaman, Y. (2015). Social media adoption: The role of media needs and innovation characteristics. *Computers in Human Behavior, 43,* 189–209.

Chapter Six

From Lesson Plans
to Marketing Plans

We see our customers as invited guests to a party, and we are the hosts. It's our job every day to make every important aspect of the customer experience a little bit better.

—Jeff Bezos, Founder of Amazon.com

Thorough lesson plans are a critical part of effective classroom practice. Detailed school improvement plans play a critical role in turning a failing school into a flourishing school. Thoughtful comprehensive needs assessments are a vital component of successful grant proposals. As a teacher, you must be able to write and implement lesson plans. As a school leader, you must be able to write and implement school improvement plans and grant proposals. In today's educational landscape, crafting a successful marketing plan is just as important. The following tools will help educators through each stage of the marketing planning process. Fully developed marketing activities should include:

- Position statement
- Market research checklist
- Marketing budget tracking sheet
- Marketing mix questionnaire
- Marketing plan template

POSITION STATEMENT DEVELOPMENT

As discussed in the marketing mix chapter, a strong positioning statement synthesizes two primary pieces of information: (1) the value your school provides to your community and (2) the perception of your school compared to other schools serving similar populations in your geographic area.

It is important to keep in mind that the value exchange focuses on how *you* define your school's value and the perception map focuses on how *others* perceive your school's value. The final positioning statement synthesizes these pieces of data to specifically name your target audience, your brand concept, and points of difference between you and your competition. Examples of value exchange propositions, perception maps, and positioning statements can be found in the marketing mix chapter of this text.

Value exchange proposition: Essential components to defining your school's value exchange with your community could include grades or ages of students served, naming the community you serve, noting any long-standing traditions, key elements from your mission statement or the strategic plan, aspirational goals for your students, and the pedagogical model you implement. Define the value you provide the community:

_____

_____

_____

_____

_____

_____

_____

Perception map: Selecting two indicators is the most important aspect of perception map creation. It is important to select these indicators based on points of interest to your community. Key indicators should be specific to data on indicators that families and students use when making choices. Examples could include academic performance, extracurricular offerings, community engagement, or staff quality. Once you have selected the two indicators that define choice making of the families and students in your

Perceptual Map

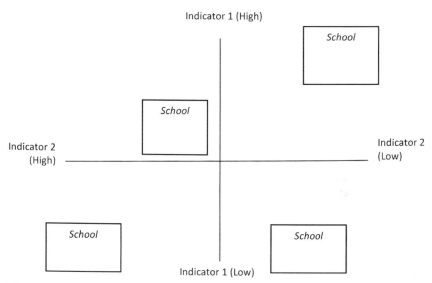

Figure 6.1. Perceptual Map

community for the *X*- and *Y*-axes of your map (Figure 6.1), fill in where your school and your competition schools fall on the map.

Synthesize the information from your value exchange proposition and your perception map into a positioning statement. Your positioning statement should include your target population, your brand concept, and points that differentiate you from your competition. Write your final positioning statement:

_____

_____

_____

_____

_____

_____

_____

MARKET RESEARCH CHECKLIST

Below is a checklist of points to keep in mind when embarking on market research. Completing this checklist prior to beginning your marketing activities will ensure that your efforts are effective and streamlined (Table 6.1).

1. Objective of research:

   _____

   _____

2. What sources will you use and what data will you collect?

   _____

   _____

3. What is your collection timeline and methods for collection?

   _____

   _____

4. What does your data say and what does it mean for your marketing efforts?

   _____

   _____

Table 6.1. Marketing Budget Tracking Sheet

Expense Category	Jul	Aug	Sept	Oct	Nov	Dec	Jan	Feb	Mar	Apr	May	Jun	Total
Marketing Research													
Primary research													
Secondary research													
Databases/licenses													
Total													$
Marketing Communication													
Advertising													
Public relations													
Direct marketing													
Events													
Sales promotion													
Website/social media													
Printing													
Other													
Total													$
Student Acquisition and Retention													
Lead generation													
Student retention													
Total													$
Other													
Postage													
Travel													
Other													
Total													
Total Marketing Budget													$

MARKETING MIX QUESTIONNAIRE

Product

1. Does the product (service), as it stands right now, meet the needs of your target customers? Yes or No

   If yes, what needs does the product meet? How specifically does the product meet those needs?

   _____

   _____

   If no, what changes or additions need to occur so that the product meets the needs of your target audience?

   _____

   _____

Price (Value)

2. What level of value do the members of your target audience assign to your product?

   _____ Tremendous value. Your product is seen as the superior option in all respects.

   Why?

   _____

   _____

   _____ Some value. Your product is viewed as comparable to other competing options.

   Why?

   _____

   _____

_____ Lesser value. Your product is viewed as somewhat less valuable than other competition options.

Why?

_____

_____

_____ Limited value. Your product is viewed as offering considerably limited value, relative to competing options.

Why?

_____

_____

3. If your value proposition is not what you hope it would be, what changes do you need to make to the product to increase the value proposition?

_____

_____

4. If your value proposition is excellent, what changes do you need to make to the other aspects of the marketing mix?

_____

_____

Place

5. Do the members of your target have easy and open access to your product? Yes or No

If no, what are three to five things you could do to improve access to the product?

_____

_____

6. Would making changes to the access to your product also allow you to reach new customers?

   Why? How?

   _____

   _____

7. What barriers or challenges must be overcome in order to improve access?

   Explain.

   _____

   _____

Promotion

8. How has this organization typically promoted this (or a similar) product?

   _____

   _____

9. Should anything from the existing, traditional strategy be dropped?

   Why?

   _____

   _____

10. What new promotional tools or strategies should you try that will help you promote this product?

    Why?

    _____

    _____

Implementation

To achieve your objective, what items need to occur (Table 6.2)?

- First brainstorm for *all* of the items or tasks that need to happen.
- Review the list, and then try to put them in a sequential order.
- Identify the person/department/function that is either responsible for the task or involved in some way.

Table 6.2

MARKETING PLAN TEMPLATE

Product: (What are you trying to promote?)

_____

Target audience: (To whom are you selling or promoting your product?)

_____

Objective: (What do you want your target audience to do?)

_____

Timeline: (How long will your activity last?)

_____

Measurement: (How will you measure the success made toward realizing your objective?)

_____

Index

Index

About the Authors

Azure D. S. Angelov has a BA in elementary and special education from Marian University, an MS in effective teaching from Butler University, and a PhD in special education and multicultural education from Indiana University, Bloomington. Additionally, Dr. Angelov completed the High Potential Leaders Executive Education program at Harvard Business School. Dr. Angelov began her career as a special education teacher and varsity coach. For 10 years, she served as an associate professor at the University of Indianapolis, earning tenure in 2011. She also served as director of research at the Indiana Department of Education, where she wrote Indiana's Quality Counts grant. Dr. Angelov has educated more than 1,500 teachers, written 42 peer-reviewed research articles and three books, earned numerous local and national honors, and brought in more than $70 million in competitive grant dollars for educational entities.

Deidre M. Pettinga, PhD, has more than 30 years of marketing experience, which runs the spectrum from applied to theoretical. On the applied side, she served as chief marketing officer for a national youth-serving nonprofit organization, vice president of client services for a marketing software company, research director for a CBS television affiliate, marketing director for a regional restaurant chain, and account executive and media buyer for an advertising agency. Her theoretical experience includes 10 years as an assistant professor of marketing at the University of Indianapolis and four years as an adjunct marketing faculty member at Butler University. Dr. Pettinga earned a BS and an MBA from Butler University, Indianapolis, Indiana, and an MA and a PhD from Fielding

Graduate University, Santa Barbara, California. She has presented to numerous business, civic, and education organizations, including the Indiana Center for Family, School and Community Partnerships, the Marketing Management Association, the American Camp Association, and the Indiana Conference of the United Methodist Church. Her articles have appeared in the *Journal of Academic Administration in Higher Education*, *Journal of the Academy of Business Education*, and the *International Journal of Motorsport Management*, and she has coauthored two other books on K–12 educational marketing.

David F. Bateman, PhD, is a professor at Shippensburg University in the Department of Educational Leadership and Special Education, where he teaches courses on special education law, assessment, and facilitating inclusion. He is a former due process hearing officer for Pennsylvania for over 580 hearings. He uses his knowledge of litigation relating to special education to assist school districts in providing appropriate supports for students with disabilities and to prevent and recover from due process hearings. He has been a classroom teacher of students with learning disabilities, behavior disorders, intellectual disability, and hearing impairments and a building administrator for summer programs. Dr. Bateman earned a PhD in special education from the University of Kansas. He has recently coauthored the following books: *A Principal's Guide to Special Education*, *A Teacher's Guide to Special Education*, *Charting the Course: Special Education in Charter Schools*, and the forthcoming *Special Education Leadership: Building Effective Programming in Schools*.